THE FARM & WILDERNESS
SUMMER CAMPS

THE FARM
& WILDERNESS
SUMMER CAMPS

Progressive Ideals in the Twentieth Century

EMILY K. ABEL AND MARGARET K. NELSON

RUTGERS UNIVERSITY PRESS
New Brunswick, Camden, and Newark, New Jersey
London and Oxford

Rutgers University Press is a department of Rutgers, The State University of New Jersey, one of the leading public research universities in the nation. By publishing worldwide, it furthers the University's mission of dedication to excellence in teaching, scholarship, research, and clinical care.

Library of Congress Cataloging-in-Publication Data

Names: Abel, Emily K., author. | Nelson, Margaret K., 1944– author.
Title: The Farm & Wilderness summer camps : progressive ideals in the twentieth century / Emily K. Abel, Margaret K. Nelson.
Other titles: Farm and Wilderness summer camps
Description: New Brunswick, New Jersey : Rutgers University Press, 2023. | Includes bibliographical references and index.
Identifiers: LCCN 2023012487 | ISBN 9781978836631 (paperback) | ISBN 9781978836648 (hardcover) | ISBN 9781978836655 (epub) | ISBN 9781978836662 (pdf)
Subjects: LCSH: Farm & Wilderness—History. | Camps—United States—History—20th century. | Camps—Social aspects—United States—History—20th century. | Youth—United States—Attitudes—History—20th century. | Social change—United States—History—20th century.
Classification: LCC GV193 .A25 2023 | DDC 796.54097309/04—dc23/eng/20230518
LC record available at https://lccn.loc.gov/2023012487

A British Cataloging-in-Publication record for this book is available from the British Library.

References to internet websites (URLs) were accurate at the time of writing. Neither the author nor Rutgers University Press is responsible for URLs that may have expired or changed since the manuscript was prepared.

♾ The paper used in this publication meets the requirements of the American National Standard for Information Sciences—Permanence of Paper for Printed Library Materials, ANSI Z39.48-1992.

rutgersuniversitypress.org

CONTENTS

CHRONOLOGY

1939	The Webbs found Timberlake (originally called Camp Mehrlicht)
1941	Indian Brook established
1947	First African American campers enrolled
1952	William (Bill) Rassenes Cook (Wakio) died
1953	Senior Work Camp / Tamarack Farm established
1953	*Summer Magic* published by Kenneth B. and Susan H. Webb
1954	Family Camp begins
1956	Peggy and Emily first attend Indian Brook
1957	Timberlake exchange program with Camp Atwater
1961	For-profit Wilderness Corporation established
1962	Saltash Mountain Camp established
1963	*The Boy Who Could Sleep When the Wind Blew* published by Kenneth B. Webb
1965	Flying Cloud established
1968	Camp Ko-Ko-Pah / renamed Dark Meadow
1969	Great Leap Backward at Flying Cloud led by Rick Hausman
1969–1970	Seaforth Camp in Virgin Gorda
1973	Webbs Retire; Farm & Wilderness Foundation formed and becomes a nonprofit; Jack Hunter is its first executive director
1973	Susan Webb joined Vermont legislature (four terms end in 1980)
1973	*As Sparks Fly Upward* published by Kenneth B. Webb
1976	Saltash Mountain Camp becomes coed; Dark Meadow closes
1977	Women at Work signs appear at Indian Brook
1978	Relationship formed with 1199 SEIU of New York City
1980s	Barn Day Camp established
1984	Death of Ken Webb
1989	*Beyond Our Wildest Dreams* published by Kenneth B. and Susan H. Webb

1990	Jack Sloanaker fired; sentenced for sexual abuse four years later
1990	Liz Ohle writes article about homophobia in *Camping Magazine*
1994	Letter sent to former Timberlake campers asking about sexual abuse
2000s	Partnership formed with Akwesasne Mohawk Tribe; Red Spruce Grove established; Long Trail Questers established
2001	Wilderness Corporation evolved into the nonprofit Ninevah Foundation
2007	End of Fifth Freedom at F&W
2011	Death of Susan Webb at age 103; honored by House Concurrent Resolution in memory of Representative Susan Webb, H.C.R. 372
2018	Ninevah Foundation and Farm & Wilderness join forces
2021	*Beyond Our Wildest Dreams* revised and updated by Kristi Webb
2022	Camp Indian Brook name changed to Firefly Song

THE FARM & WILDERNESS
SUMMER CAMPS

INTRODUCTION

Old camp newspapers take us back to our summers as girls and teens. Peggy and a cabinmate win a three-legged race. Peggy's "pet passion" is "candy on trips"; her "pet peeve" is "going the second mile." When asked how she feels about her sister Emily, she punts, asking, "What did she say?" Emily responds more generously to the same question, saying simply, "I love her." Emily's name appears frequently as editor and illustrator, reminding us how she avoids the camp's more arduous activities. Our friends, siblings, and Peggy's husband ("Billy Nelson is also very popular") appear in their juvenile guises.

We are reading these mimeographed sheets because we have just begun to conduct research on Farm & Wilderness (F&W), the group of Vermont private summer camps first founded in 1939 by Susan H. Webb and Kenneth B. Webb. A sociologist (Peggy) and historian (Emily) as well as sisters, we have recently finished writing a biography of the African American woman who cared for us and our three other siblings as children.[1] If Mable Jones provided the warmth and security we needed when we were very young, Farm & Wilderness served as a refuge for us as older children and teenagers contending with the politics, culture, and social pressures of the 1950s and early 1960s. Together, we attended Indian Brook (IB), the girls' camp, in 1956 and 1957; separately, we went to Tamarack Farm (TF), the coed camp for young teens, and then returned to Indian Brook as counselors. At other times, our older sister, younger brothers, a few of our children, and assorted nieces and nephews spent summers at various F&W camps. Unfortunately, not all of them were as happy there as we had been. Ours might have been a very special time in the history of F&W.

In the context of the post–World War II era, F&W promoted unusual ideals. These included simplicity, cooperation, a spirituality based in nature, a rejection of the confining strictures of 1950s femininity, racial integration, and an orientation toward pacifism. Our initial writing plan was to demonstrate how the camps provided a haven for the offspring of parents like ours who supported those ideals. As we looked more closely, however, we discovered that the camps reproduced as well as resisted prevailing cultural norms. The more interesting story, we now understood, was how the camps struggled to adapt the founders' ideals to changing understandings of race and ethnicity, social class, gender, and sexual orientation. We thus decided to write a social history of the camps between 1939 and the last part of the twentieth century, exploring them within the context of the times and examining how they responded to shifts in culture and society. In some cases, the camps took a leadership role; in other cases, they lagged behind other organizations. Our book serves as a case study of the uneven pace of institutional change.

A central theme in the history of childhood is the establishment of special spaces for children.[2] The first U.S. summer camps appeared in the 1880s. By the post–World War II era, known as "the golden age of American childhood," hundreds of summer camps for children dotted the Northeast.[3] We began our investigation of F&W by examining summer camps in general. We read scores of personal accounts and spoke with numerous adults. These all attested to the enormous power camps have over children. Former campers write and speak joyfully about the strong bonds they forged, their sense of being at their best (and better than they were at home), acquiring new skills, feeling appreciated (often for the first time), and finding relief from family conflicts and tensions. Of course, some children are homesick or bullied, never get used to the bugs and the dark, or find themselves at odds with the camp's orientation.[4] However, most accounts, including those in young adult literature, report that summer camps engender friendships, help children recognize their own strengths, and teach them that they can survive (and be seen as) independent of their families. Psychological and social psychological studies confirm these testimonials. Children who attend summer camps for periods ranging from short stays to two months show increased self-esteem, social skills, independence, and environmental awareness. Moreover, these positive developmental outcomes extend well beyond those that might be expected by maturation alone.[5]

When we turned to the social science literature about camps, we were stunned to discover how thin it was. The few sociologists who discuss summer camps tend to employ the notion of total institutions. First described by Erving Goffman in *Asylums*, total institutions are places where a large number of people live together for a length of time, cut off from the wider community. All aspects of life (sleep, play, eating, and work) occur in the same location and in the company of others and are planned "to fulfill the official aims of the institution"; the staff remain separate from the "inmates." According to Goffman, these institutions are "forcing houses for changing persons: each is a natural experiment on what can be done to the self."[6] Although most commentators acknowledge that summer camps do not fit precisely into Goffman's conceptual apparatus, the notion of total institutions helps explain how camps can exert such a profound influence on children.

Anthropologists add two other concepts. One is "liminality." In liminal spaces (as in total institutions), individuals are separated from all that is familiar and freed from the constraints and structures of everyday life. The emergence of what Victor Turner calls "communitas," a sense of "spontaneous connection or group feeling that people in a social situation feel toward each other and the group," is especially likely in liminal situations because individuals cannot retreat into—and are freed from being recognized as members of—their everyday associations.[7] The second is ritual. Anthropologists define rituals as acts or series of acts repeated regularly by important people in a precise manner and specific places. Rituals help set off the "sacred" from the "profane" or "ordinary" and help create "communitas."

All three concepts can easily be applied to summer camps: children live away from their families, depend on other campers for sociability and support, and participate in predictable group activities that differ from those they enjoy at home. As a result, they become different people, members of a new (albeit temporary) society. Given the relevance of these concepts, it is surprising that most sociologists and anthropologists ignore summer camps entirely. In both books and journal articles, school and home take pride of place as explanations for children's development.

Although three excellent histories of summer camps exist, none extends beyond 1960; moreover, they leave many issues unaddressed. Leslie Paris's fascinating, wide-ranging, and well-researched *Children's Nature: The Rise of the American Summer Camp* ends in 1940, the year after our story begins; *A Manufactured Wilderness: Summer Camps and the Shaping of American Youth, 1890–1960*, by Abigail A. Van Slyck, focuses primarily on the landscape and built environment; and as its title indicates, *The Nurture of Nature: Childhood, Antimodernism, and Ontario Summer Camps, 1920–55*, by Sharon Wall, excludes U.S. summer camps. General histories of children emphasize families and schools but say little about how young people spend their summer months.[8] Steven Mintz's monumental 2004 book, *Huck's Raft: A History of American Childhood*, for example, lacks an entry for camps in the index and pays virtually no attention to them.[9]

Farm & Wilderness between 1939 and 1999 resembled most other private camps in the same period in various ways. The former campers and counselors we spoke to echoed many of the themes that emerged in novels, analytic accounts, and the personal testimonies we had read. Those who returned year after year emphasized the special relationships they formed, the activities that were available, and the opportunity for personal growth. Like campers elsewhere, they enjoyed being away from the routines of ordinary life and trying on new selves in new surroundings. They reveled in the rituals, which confirmed membership in the group. At Farm & Wilderness, those included the bonfire on the Fourth of July, campfire singing, square dances, hayrides, the annual fair, and the banquet marking the end of the season. One former camper described her summers at Indian Brook in rapturous language, recalling "the excitement, the bliss, the romance of being at last among one's own people—the piney grassy smell of camp, the walk along the road to a square dance, the view of the mountains from the IB dock ('I will lift up mine eyes unto the hills, from whence cometh my help'), listening to Beethoven on the lawn around the IB lodge, a feeling of possibility, and a feeling of being seen."[10]

To the extent that the camps the Webbs founded can be considered representative of children's camps in general, this book helps fill a major gap in the history and sociology of America's youth in the second half of the twentieth century. But the Farm & Wilderness camps also had some distinctive features, which, although not entirely unique, have received little historical attention in other writings about summer camps.

Farm & Wilderness encouraged different generations of campers to engage in political activism that was considered progressive in different eras. The leaders' commitment to social justice also led them to try to diversify F&W in terms of race, social class, and sexual orientation before most other private camps did. With few examples to guide them, the leadership had to find ways to respond to the needs of very different groups of campers. Although affiliated with the Quakers and remembered by many alumni as a profoundly spiritual place, Farm & Wilderness differed from Jewish and other Christian camps in enrolling children who came from many different faith traditions. It had a daily Quaker-style silent meeting for worship but did not provide religious instruction or require religious observance other than attendance at the meeting.

Some distinctive features complicated the efforts to achieve social justice and thus represent another reason we chose to write about them. We can see this especially with nudism. Ken Webb espoused freedom from clothes, which he called the "Fifth Freedom," thereby elevating it to the lofty realm of the four freedoms (freedom of speech, freedom of worship, freedom from want, and freedom from fear), which President Franklin D. Roosevelt articulated in 1941. For all Ken's advocacy, the practice was never as widespread as generally assumed, and it was finally eliminated in 2007. Understandably, however, it is the topic that emerges most often when Peggy mentions F&W to friends, colleagues, and casual acquaintances in Vermont. "Oh," they say, "you went to the 'nudist' camp." The "Fifth Freedom" also attracted the most negative attention in the local newspapers and the surrounding community. Most significantly, as we discuss in chapter 5, it may well have made more likely or even provided the underpinnings for the occasional sex abuse of campers by counselors that occurred at one of the camps in the second half of the twentieth century. And until it was banned, it limited the camp's clientele.

Other distinctive characteristics have tended to loom much larger in the memories of the members of the F&W community we spoke to. Like all summer camps, Farm & Wilderness was (and continues to be) situated in what historian Abigail Van Slyck calls a "manufactured" wilderness, an environment that is partially and carefully cultivated to allow for cabins, lodges, and campfire rings. But F&W insisted that it disturbed nature less than other camps did and that it exposed children more thoroughly to the elements. Mindy Thompson Fullilove, from her perspective as a professor of clinical psychiatry and public health, recalled that other camps she saw as both a camper and parent "attempt to civilize a bit of land, and that is where the cabins are erected. Nature is only present to provide cool breezes and a nice lake. That was not the Webbs' idea of how to build a camp. They attempted to hide the camps in the woods. Nature, in the form of bugs and trees and the elements, is everywhere at F&W."[11] Both campers and staff took pride in the special ruggedness of the built environment. They also glorified the exceptional rigor of the camping trips and work projects. That rigor, like nudism, made F&W attractive only to some campers and staff.

So far we have discussed Farm & Wilderness as a unit, but the individual camps had distinct histories and goals and served different groups. They also had different strengths and weaknesses. Originally called "Mehrlicht," Timberlake (TL), the boys' camp, opened on the northern end of Woodward Reservoir in 1939 (just before the outbreak of World War II) with twenty-eight campers. Two years later, Indian Brook (IB, now known as Firefly Song), the girls' camp, began on the opposite end of the lake with twelve campers. By the mid-1950s, each camp had an enrollment of 115.[12] The coed Senior Work Camp (later called Tamarack Farm) for young adolescents opened in 1953, on the lakefront midway between Timberlake and Indian Brook. Two "outpost" camps for boys were established on Lake Ninevah, eleven miles from the rest of F&W, in the 1960s—Saltash Mountain Camp (SAM), emphasizing hiking and forestry, in 1962, and Flying Cloud (FC), stressing "Indian lore," in 1964. Ko-Ko-Pah, for girls, was established on an Adirondack lake in 1968. The following year, it was moved to a site near Lake Ninevah and renamed Dark Meadow. When that camp closed in 1976, SAM became coed. Camp Seaforth, on the British Virgin Islands, had an even shorter life-span. It operated only in the summers of 1969 and 1970. Family Camp, providing opportunities for families to spend a week at F&W at the end of the regular summer session, opened in 1954. In the past few decades, F&W added the Barn Day Camp (for children four to ten), Red Spruce Grove (an "off-the-grid" summer camp for female and nongender binary campers eleven to fourteen), and the Questers (a hiking and backpacking camp for teens), which did not reopen after the pandemic. Although the individual camps continue to serve different groups, they share the same philosophy and goals.

FIGURE 1. Cabin in the woods at Indian Brook. Photograph courtesy of Margaret Nelson.

Today, the F&W website lists its values as "Simplicity, Peace, Integrity, Community, Equity, and Sustainability."

During the years Ken and Susan Webb directed Farm & Wilderness, they located campers by traveling to communities, primarily in the Northeast, where they knew they could find interested families. In the 1960s, they also visited the

South to recruit both Black and White campers. In addition, they advertised the camps in parents' magazines, the *New York Times,* and the *Friends Journal.* Their outreach efforts produced applications primarily from parents who were middle- and upper-middle class. Ken asserted that the publicity surrounding his early efforts at integration helped him attract a clientele that shared his ideals. Recently, F&W hired a communications firm to create an advertising campaign for the camps.[13] These advertisements can be found on LinkedIn, Facebook, Yelp, Twitter, and local websites like Park Slope Parents in Brooklyn.

Because the camps depended entirely on fees, they struggled financially for many years. When the Webbs ceded control to the nonprofit Farm & Wilderness Foundation in 1973, the camps were on the verge of collapse. The somewhat foolhardy Seaforth venture had produced an enormous debt, and the Webbs had deferred essential maintenance on the other camps. The financial arrangement with the Webbs on their retirement added another stress. The new corporation agreed to pay off the mortgage on the land and buildings the Webbs had owned. The size of the mortgage itself was based on an appraisal of the "highest and best use" for the property, which assumed the possibility of development on the land on a beautiful lake near a prime skiing area. It thus far exceeded the actual value of the property if it were to continue to be the location of the three summer camps situated there. Although the Webbs never charged the full amount of the appraisal (though according to Len Cadwallader, who became the business director in 1976, something like approximately half of it), they depended on regular payments for their own well-being and pensions.[14] But even to pay that reduced amount left the nonprofit scrambling. Having gone through one line of credit, the corporation was paying heavy interest rates on a second. Now the lack of maintenance had begun to show. Cadwallader (who moved into the position of executive director in 1985 and remained in that role for twenty-one years) remembered rain falling into buckets in the Indian Brook lodge during storms. Fortunately, Cadwallader was able to put the camps on steadier financial footing. In the 1980s, that newfound stability teetered when the dam on Woodward Reservoir failed and had a multimillion-dollar price tag for rebuilding it. A campaign, with the motto "Give a dam," garnered sufficient funds from loyal alumni and other supporters to save the camps. Although reports of sexual abuse in the 1990s again threatened the camps' existence, they managed to survive and even flourish again.

Our research on Farm & Wilderness took various forms. We interviewed forty-two people, including ex-campers, staff, directors, and board members. Many individuals had had multiple roles, and many had remained affiliated with F&W for long periods of time as they enrolled their own children and grandchildren in the camps.[15] Those interviews typically lasted an hour, and most were recorded and transcribed. Each person quoted here by name gave permission

to use written and oral materials. In two cases, we have given people pseud-
onyms (indicated as such at the first mention) and have changed some details
about their lives to protect their privacy. In addition, we read the few published
memoirs by members of the Farm & Wilderness community we located and
the voluminous writings of Kenneth B. and Susan H. Webb. Their 1989 book,
Beyond Our Wildest Dreams, provided the essential background information we
needed.[16] The second edition, revised and updated by the Webbs' granddaughter
Kristi Webb in 2021, was equally valuable.[17]

We also drew on the camp archives that were available to us. Nate Hausman,
who had directed Flying Cloud from 2004 to 2006, following in the footsteps of
his father (Rick Hausman) and uncle (Bob Hausman), shared vital documents.
John Bancroft provided material related to sex abuse at Timberlake. The camps
lent us many old issues of camp newspapers, especially between the 1940s and
1980s, that had been preserved. The *Interim* was published three times during
the winter months and reported such topics as changes in leadership, births, mar-
riages, and deaths among current and former campers and the events planned
for the coming season. These were archived online from the Winter 2005–2006
to Spring 2020 issues. In hard (and musty) copy, we had access to Timberlake's *Thunderbird*, published weekly during the eight weeks of summer, Indian
Brook's *Lightning Bug*, also released every week, and Tamarack Farm's *SEWOCA*,
typically issued once a summer. These three newspapers were all essentially similar: each edition reported activities (e.g., topics for current events, work projects completed), hiking and canoe trips (especially as the summer progressed),
and cabin events. The final edition of each of these publications described each
individual camper (e.g., pet peeves and pet passions, accomplishments, favorite sayings) and provided addresses so campers could remain in touch during
the school year. Campers also volunteered creative writings and drawings. Some
of the artwork for covers and illustrations reveal a talented pool of campers. So
too do some of the short stories, poems, and humorous pieces included in these
various publications. And usually a camp director (Ken, Susan, and subsequent
directors at IB and TL as well as those at the other camps) wrote an essay on a
topic of relevance at that moment.

We were also initially provided access to unpublished material, including
directors' reports, letters by and to staff members, and other internal documents in the archives of Indian Brook and Dark Meadow. When we requested
similar material for the other camps, we were told that although the executive committee of the F&W Board was "supportive of F&W sharing with [us]
those documents in [its] archive that are in the public domain, such as news-
letters, brochures, etc.," it would no longer share "internal management documents, such as Directors' reports." Our formerly congenial relationship with the

F&W leadership deteriorated when, as a courtesy, we submitted an earlier draft of this manuscript, and we were threatened with a lawsuit if we included the internal documents they had initially given us. Although the major explanation offered was our request to use in some modified form (without attribution to any individual) some of the unpublished material, it has become clear to us the leadership was unwilling to cede control over the telling of the F&W story. They promised not to edit any drafts we showed them, but they repeatedly asked us to remove our personal tone and modify our conclusions.[18] We were charged with having made a shift in the scope of the work, although we had provided the leadership with a clear statement of our intent as soon as we realized it might have been misinterpreted.[19] Nothing we saw in the documents reflected badly on the camps. In fact, without those records, we were forced to retract some of the positive points we made in the first draft.

The chapters ahead examine different aspects of the five overnight Farm & Wilderness camps established before 2000. We focus on the 1950s and 1960s, the period we knew the camps best. In that period, Indian Brook and Timberlake were the most prominent; we thus emphasize them. (We also devote a chapter largely to Flying Cloud, and we follow a few topics beyond our cutoff point.) Because Ken and Susan Webb founded Farm & Wilderness and directed the camps for many years, chapter 1 focuses on them. Although they came from very different backgrounds and had very distinctive personalities, they agreed on basic ideals. They derived these ideals from a wide variety of disparate sources including the Bible and religious leaders, John Dewey and other philosophers, the study of Greek and Latin, their Quaker faith, and their experiences as teachers and camp directors. Confident they had established the best possible kind of camps, the Webbs published numerous popular books and magazine articles to encourage others to follow their lead.

The following chapter examines one of the distinctive aspects of Farm & Wilderness. Although virtually all camps extol the virtues of ruggedness, Farm & Wilderness went farther than most in eliminating creature comforts. The cabins were roughhewn and open to the elements and lacked running water and electricity. The hikes, canoe trips, and work projects required unusual strength and stamina. As we will see in chapter 2, some campers refused to rise to the challenges presented; others, however, enjoyed "roughing it" and took pride in their accomplishments. A few individuals we interviewed still drew on the hiking and campcraft skills they had honed decades earlier.

Activities aimed at the minds of campers complemented the demands placed on their bodies. Chapter 3 focuses first on the 1950s and 1960s, when folk music, weekly current events sessions, and ongoing discussions exposed campers to politics then considered progressive. Many people we spoke with traced their lifelong political commitments to their F&W experiences. The chapter also demonstrates that the daily meetings for worship introduced campers to a kind of spirituality that was otherwise absent from many of their lives. Although most of those we interviewed do not consider themselves Quakers, several had incorporated elements from the silent meetings at F&W into their spiritual practices. Former campers also spoke of the significant friendships they had formed as campers at F&W. Most added that as adults, they had retained some of those connections.

Chapter 4 examines the different ways Timberlake and Indian Brook approached gender issues. Under Ken's leadership, Timberlake fostered some traditional elements of masculinity, seeking to promote physical competence and keep boys away from the softening influence of women and girls. However, it offered no organized sports (except, perhaps, informal games of soccer and volleyball) and emphasized cooperation rather than competitiveness and aggression. Indian Brook under Susan's direction was an implicitly feminist environment, providing girls with opportunities to enlarge their sense of what they could do and become. As the women's movement strengthened in the 1970s, the camp became explicitly feminist. Posting "women at work" signs around camp, counselors helped girls acquire skills previously considered the exclusive province of men. In the 1980s, Indian Brook led the rest of Farm & Wilderness as well as the broader camp movement in dealing openly with the topic of sexual orientation.

In the early 1990s, reports of the sexual abuse that had occurred at Timberlake since the 1950s shattered our nostalgic image of Farm and Wilderness as a utopian society. Chapter 5 seeks to place the incidents in a broader context by exploring how and why child molestation remained undetected in large numbers of institutions for many years. We also examine the immediate response of the F&W leadership. (The conclusion reviews the subsequent reforms enacted to ensure such abuse never again could happen at the camps.)

Chapter 6 begins by examining the history of camp integration in America to demonstrate how unusual and even courageous the Webbs were. F&W were some of the first private camps to become racially integrated when the Webbs recruited a few middle-class African Americans in 1947. We then examine how later directors struggled to adapt to a larger and more diverse group of Black campers, some of whom vehemently opposed the Webbs' "color-blind" approach.

Writing in 1989, the Webbs acknowledged that they had known from the outset that most families could not easily afford F&W's fees.[20] Chapter 7 demonstrates that they tried to achieve at least some economic diversity through partial or complete scholarships based on need. The allocation of what came to be called "camperships" continued under subsequent directors. Like racial diversity, economic diversity posed its own challenges.

Ken Webb frequently expressed his admiration for Native Americans. Chapter 8 notes that in the 1940s and 1950s, he enlisted a few Native American men and several hobbyists to teach "Indian lore" to campers. He then launched a new F&W camp, Flying Cloud, modeled almost entirely on what were assumed to be Native American traditions. Long after F&W sought to respond to the criticisms of Black activists about its racial policies, boys continued to "play Indian" at Flying Cloud. At the turn of the twenty-first century, counselors and campers finally confronted the notion of cultural appropriation and gradually eliminated all trappings of Indian culture.

One former camper told us that he returned to Farm & Wilderness year after year because it incorporated "essential values." Not simply a place where kids enjoyed "running around in the woods," the camps had a "spiritual core . . . with steel in the middle of it."[21] Our book explores how successive generations of directors, counselors, and campers struggled—sometimes succeeding and sometimes failing—to adapt those values to new political understandings and transformations in the surrounding culture and society.

1 · THE FOUNDERS

Susan H. and Kenneth B. Webb founded Farm & Wilderness and directed the camps for many years. Because subsequent directors sought to remain true to the Webbs' values and vision, we begin with them. They came from very different backgrounds to meet over a shared love of classical languages, nature, spirituality, and progressive education.

On both his maternal and paternal sides, Ken's family was part of the skilled working class. His father, Francis Lincoln ("Frank") Webb, and his mother, Alma Victoria Smith, met in Springfield, Massachusetts, where both were working as printers/compositors.[1] Frank's father, Charles B. Webb, had also been a printer.[2] Alma's father was first a baker and then a butcher; her mother had been a hairdresser before her marriage.[3] Frank and Alma's only child, Kenneth B. Webb, was born in Springfield, Massachusetts, in 1902 and grew up across the river in the county of Agawam. His high school principal discovered his intellectual ability and insisted that he apply to Harvard University. After graduating in 1924, Ken taught at the American University of Beirut and started Camp Snobar in Syria but returned to the United States after a year because his father was ill and needed his help. Ken subsequently taught in Springfield (close to home), in France, and at the Peddie School in New Jersey.[4] After Ken's father died in 1934, his mother became a live-in housekeeper for an elderly man; in 1940, she earned $250/year (the same amount as the cost of a summer at F&W that year).[5] In 1944, she moved to live with Ken and Susan in Woodstock, Vermont; for a short time, she was a "companion" to an elderly woman. She died in 1961.[6]

Susan's family was considerably wealthier and better educated. Most of the men (as well as Susan's mother) had professional occupations. Her father, Harry Stinson Howard, was first a lawyer and then a judge in Burlington, Vermont. In her autobiography, Susan wrote that her mother's father, Gustave Hertz, came from Germany to work in his uncle's bank; Gustave's mother was a first cousin of the poet Heinrich Heine.[7] The census records on Ancestry.com, however, indicate that it was her great-grandfather, Gustave Hertz, who was married to Anna Heine. Susan's grandfather was Ludwig Ferdinand Hertz; her grandmother,

Mary Ann Henderson, was the daughter of the Reverend Isaac James Henderson, who had come from Scotland and studied at Princeton. The pair married in 1866. Their third child, Sue Emma Hertz (Susan's mother), was born in 1869 in New York.[8] On her father's side, Susan was descended from Oliver Otis Howard, who was appointed head of the Freedmen's Bureau at the end of the Civil War. Later, he founded Howard University and was its third president. The university was named in his honor. Susan often attributed her dedication to racial justice to this grandfather's influence.[9]

It is likely that Susan's commitment to women's equality stemmed from her mother's example. At a time when most medical schools excluded women, Sue Emma Hertz received her first medical degree from New York Women's Medical College and another from the University of Michigan in 1900. She then practiced in New York before moving to Colorado. Because an older physician there disliked having a woman doctor and made her life difficult, she wrote to Governor Ormsbee of Vermont, whom she had known from family vacations. At his suggestion, she moved to Burlington, where she worked for the Elizabeth Lund Home (for unwed mothers) and the Providence Orphan Society. She also advocated for women's suffrage (despite her husband's opposition). Susan remembered watching her mother speaking to groups of women about the importance of their right to vote. Adhering to the expectations of the times, Susan's mother stopped working as a doctor in 1908 when her identical twin daughters were born. But she returned as soon as she could. When the girls started school, she became the physician for all the Burlington public schools. Susan remembered the day her mother got that appointment: "Harriet and I came home from school to be greeted by a very delighted smiling mother."[10]

After their marriage in 1932, Ken and Susan Webb moved to Cambridge, Massachusetts, where Ken studied for his MA at Harvard University. Unable to afford more education for Ken, the young couple returned to Agawam, where they lived for a year in an apartment on the third floor of Ken's mother's house. They then moved to Saxton's River, Vermont, where Ken taught at the Vermont Academy. From there, they moved to the Park School in Buffalo. Ken opened Camp Mehrlicht (later renamed Timberlake) in 1939 and cofounded the Woodstock Country Day School in 1944.[11] Although he remained involved in the Woodstock Country Day School for less than two years, he never relinquished the goal of establishing an independent Quaker school.

Susan and Ken had three children, all of whom spent years involved with F&W and had professional careers. Susan (Sukie) Webb Hammond, a political scientist who taught at American University, was born in 1933 and died in 2016. The Webbs' only son, Robert (Bob) Howard Webb, was born in 1934 and died in 2018. Like his father, Bob graduated from Harvard University. After obtaining a PhD from Rutgers University, he was affiliated with Schepens Eye Research

Institute and Wellman Laboratory at Massachusetts, where he invented diagnostic medical instrumentation.[12] Bob's wife, Charme, worked at Indian Brook for many years and, at one time, was an assistant director while Susan, her mother-in-law, was the director. The Webbs' third child, Martha (Miki) Webb, was born in 1941; she worked for many years as a doctor and currently lives in Las Cruces. Like her siblings, she sent children and then grandchildren to F&W.

SHARED PHILOSOPHY

We are fortunate to have many publications by the Webbs that elucidate their philosophy. Although both Ken and Susan are listed as the authors of *Summer Magic: What Children Gain from Camp* (1953) and *The Boy Who Could Sleep When the Wind Blew* (1963), the writing is in Ken's style, and we assume he was the primary author.[13] He alone wrote the 1973 book *As Sparks Fly Upward: The Rationale of the Farm and Wilderness Camps* and a 1989 biography for adults and young readers, *From Plymouth Notch to President: The Farm Boyhood of Calvin Coolidge*.[14] Ken and Susan together wrote a few articles in popular magazines in the later 1950s and 1960s, but Ken was the sole author of many more. The title page of *Beyond Our Wildest Dreams: The Story of the Farm and Wilderness Camps, 1939–1989* (first edition) also names both Ken and Susan as authors.[15] However, throughout the book, Susan Webb speaks in the first person. For example, the introduction opens with these words: "As I look back over the years I am amazed that Farm and Wilderness exists. How could we have considered Ken's breaking off from a successful teaching career in someone else's school and starting our own educational adventure. But Ken wanted a school of his own for so long."[16] (In what follows, we refer to both Webbs as having written the book unless Susan speaks in the first person.) In 2021, when Kristi Webb updated this book, she made some significant changes: she removed all mention of an individual known to have been involved in sexual predation, and she altered some of the language to suit current norms.[17]

In *Beyond Our Wildest Dreams*, the Webbs wrote that they based the camp on Quaker principles, which they defined as "simplicity, social concern, and the search for spiritual truth."[18] The daily meetings for worship were "the soul of the camp." Although Susan traced her commitment to racial justice to her family history, she also referred to their adoption of the Quaker faith: "We had become members of the Religious Society of Friends (usually known as Quakers) several years earlier while Ken was teaching in Baltimore, but even before that the testimonies of the Friends' simplicity, concern for each other, and peace, spoke to our condition."[19] Founded in 1917, the American Friends Service Committee (AFSC) had long provided a practical expression of Quaker ideals. Although the original goal was to offer conscientious objectors an alternative to military

FIGURE 2. Kenneth and Susan Webb. Photograph courtesy of William Boardman.

service in World War I, the committee soon expanded its work both nationally and internationally. Numerous observers have noted that the AFSC did not reflect the views of a majority of Quakers; that by the 1950s, less than a third of its permanent staff identified as Quakers; and that many Quaker schools and meetings resisted integration for many years.[20] Nevertheless, the AFSC offered a model of social justice activism that the Webbs could emulate. In 1947, the committee was one of two groups awarded the Nobel Peace Prize for work among Asian Americans during World War II. It provided emotional and material support to those in internment camps, protected their property, and found them temporary housing after their return. In addition, the committee helped remove approximately 3,600 students from the camps and send them to colleges and universities.[21] The AFSC also had a long history of promoting equal rights for African Americans. As we will see in chapter 6, that history appears to have informed the Webbs' efforts to create an interracial camp in the 1940s.

Because the Quakers represented a tiny fraction of the U.S. population, the Webbs might have had little influence in camp circles had they relied solely on that religious group for inspiration. They gained prominence by also expressing ideas that were far more widespread. Especially in the post–World War II period, those included an emphasis on the therapeutic value of summer camps.[22] The late 1940s and 1950s were the golden age of psychotherapy. Membership in both the American Psychological Association and the American Psychiatric Association soared.[23] Ken argued that "in the intimate relations of a camp, where adults of understanding and skill may bring a detached, objective point of view to a youngster's problem, the boy or girl who is groping for something he doesn't comprehend is often started on the road to self realization. Whether it is some emotional tangle or just the drifter who hasn't yet found himself, the chances of his waking up—'getting wise to himself,' as youth puts it—are better in the new and challenging environment of a camp than they are in any other place."[24]

Ken offered numerous examples of children who returned home at the end of the summer not only physically stronger but also more resourceful, responsible, generous, and self-assured. "The changes were immediately evident" with a boy he called Bill. "A member of one of today's big families, Bill had been caught in the swirl of sibling rivalry." His parents were understanding but could not give him help within the family: "The only effective antidote was separation for a summer, an antidote that proved to be invaluable." He returned "with a new appreciation for his brother, Ed." In addition, "Bill had lost his habit of nagging his sister Anne."[25] Another boy had become more tolerant of his parents and more willing to communicate with them.[26] Conforming to the professional expertise of the 1950s, Ken placed his greatest emphasis on cultivating social adjustment, the ability to accommodate the demands and mores of society and to form satisfying and harmonious relationships with others. He wrote that when parents were asked what they most wanted their child to derive from camp, "the answer frequently is that they want him 'to learn how to get along with others.'" The best counselors taught their campers how to fit in with the group and make others like them.[27]

The Webbs wrote in 1989 that they also believed "strongly" in the progressive education movement associated with John Dewey.[28] Although Dewey is remembered primarily for his impact on schools, he also had a powerful effect on summer camps. In planning Farm & Wilderness, the Webbs were able to seek guidance from other directors who had sought to incorporate progressive education principles. They also may have consulted *Creative Camping* by Joshua Lieberman, one of the most widely read books in the camping movement in the 1930s. Lieberman based his account on his experience as a camp director when he had adopted a "child-centered" approach to replace the rigid management style of earlier camps.[29]

Resting on an optimistic view of children's potential, progressive education programs in both schools and camps sought to equip children for democracy by emphasizing cooperation, flexibility, practical skills, and experiential learning.[30] Fostering democracy was a critical concern to Ken Webb as well. In a 1951 article titled "Many a Camp Democratically Run, with Campers Taking Part," he extolled "the democratic spirit of give and take in the camp, the easy comradery, [and] the absence of artificial dignity on the part of the counselors."[31] Ken also frequently expressed his high regard for children's innate qualities. They "take naturally to the ideal of simplicity and rugged living," "have a sense of awe and wonder," demonstrate creativity in many areas, and are free of racial prejudice.[32] Lambasting the traditional nature study programs that relied on rote memorization, Ken urged directors to devise games that engaged children's imaginations. At Farm & Wilderness, he insisted that campers acquire the practical skills they needed for hiking trips and work projects. Above all, Ken stressed the need for cooperation. He contrasted the unhealthy "competition for school standing or athletic excellence" that children experienced throughout the academic year with the "more wholesome challenge" they found at camps when "all benefit together, none at the expense of others." On camping trips, when "the testing of the storm or the mountain or the stretch of white water has been met and overcome, all rejoice together, with a comradeship of tried and true friendship. These youngsters know each other's weaknesses and make allowance, seeing these foibles perhaps as a reflection of their own. But they also know each other's strength. Their safety has depended on these strengths; to respect is added gratitude."[33]

In addition, like many camp directors, the Webbs expressed views that resonated with those of two other movements that emerged at the turn of the twentieth century. Together, they explain the name "Farm & Wilderness." The first movement sought to designate certain land as national parks to safeguard them from the encroachment of "civilization." Frederick Jackson Turner's 1893 essay on the closing of the frontier generated fear that the wilderness that had shaped the unique American character was in danger of disappearing.[34] The writer Owen Wister described the postfrontier society as "a shapeless state, a condition of men and manners as unlovely as is that moment in the year when winter is gone and spring not come, and the face of Nature is ugly."[35] Ken viewed wilderness hikes as a way to redeem some of what had been lost. One of the badges Farm & Wilderness offered for achievements in campcraft was "the Pioneer." In *Summer Magic*, he wrote that "the keenest thrill attends exploration trips, where the trail is new to most of the hikers, or where an experienced group strikes off through the pathless wilderness with only a map and compass to guide them."[36] *As Sparks Fly Upward* described Timberlake's Explorer Club, which sponsored various expeditions. The name, he wrote, has the "advantage of romance: it suggests far-off places, a dash of danger; and adventure with strange new forms of wildlife."[37] The boys "who have shown they can take it are sent out with a top-flight campcraft man and some assistant leader. They carry little beyond moccasins, a knife and breech cloth, matches, fish hooks, a blanket, and a few raisins, hunks of cheese and some dried apricots. They 'bushwack' or they make their way to some known camping spot and devote themselves to just staying alive." They return "with a bit of swagger and endless tales of adventure." The bravest boys set out for the wilderness alone.[38]

Along with their descendants and supporters, the Webbs also participated more directly in the campaign to preserve the wilderness by purchasing land near F&W whenever it became available. Some of the earliest acquisitions included the cabins at Indian Brook, known as Birches and Beaver Lodge. Ken and Susan's son, Bob, helped with the creation of "Plymouth Community North," a collection of houses at the north end of Woodward Reservoir across Route 100.[39] And in 1961, the Webbs expanded their land ownership to nearby Mount Holly when, with the help of a group of supporters, they bought a 310-acre wooded tract on the eastern side of Lake Ninevah for $20,000.[40] Several years later, the group formed the Wilderness Corporation with Ken Webb as president, Jack Sloanaker as vice president, Susan Webb as secretary, and Charles Harvey as treasurer. Eventually, the Wilderness Corporation acquired, and protected from development, almost 3,000 acres.[41]

A second movement encouraged Americans to abandon cities for the countryside. Although we tend to associate homesteading with the counter-culture of the late 1960s and 1970s, back-to-the-land projects were launched as soon as the United States shifted from an agrarian to an urban nation. The proportion of Americans living in rural areas declined from two-thirds in 1890 to slightly more than half by 1910. Forty-three percent of Americans were farmers in 1890, but less than a third were by 1910.[42] Like the looming disappearance of the wilderness, this change aroused fears that the nation's most basic identity was at risk. In the late nineteenth and early twentieth centuries, a wide variety of writers—including socialists, Jewish leaders, participants in the arts and crafts movement, and single taxers—urged Americans to leave the cities to take up farming. Many men and some women heeded that call.[43]

By the 1920s, the impulse to move to the country had largely faded. But then, as part of the 1930s New Deal, the Department of the Interior's Division of Subsistence Homesteads placed low-income industrial workers on small plots of land where they could produce some of their own food.[44] Simultaneously, a few professionals moved to Vermont to farm. The most famous were Scott and Helen Nearing. Born in 1883, Scott Nearing was a blacklisted academic in 1932 when he and his much younger wife, Helen, decided to buy a dilapidated farmhouse and land in Jamaica, Vermont, and become farmers. They remained there until 1952, when they left for Maine.[45] Norm Williams, a major figure at Farm & Wilderness between 1953 and 1966, worked on the Nearings' farm before coming to the camps.[46]

Although virtually all camps rest on the assumption that, especially for children, country life is vastly superior to city life, historian Michael B. Smith argues that Ken stood out for his antipathy to urban environments.[47] In fact, Ken directed his animus toward suburbs as well as cities. After World War II, large numbers of Americans moved to suburban communities, where growing prosperity and government programs enabled them to buy single-family houses and fill them with consumer goods. Suburbanites represented 19.5 percent of the population in 1940 and 30.7 percent by 1960.[48] Consumerism was now patriotic. "The good purchaser devoted to 'more, newer and better' was a good citizen," wrote historian Lizabeth Cohen.[49]

William Levitt and other developers built affordable suburban homes for families with small incomes, but Ken assumed his campers came primarily from the most affluent communities. "Plush" was an adjective he frequently attached to the word "suburbs." He complained that women's departure from the workforce combined with the availability of labor-saving devices meant that children had few chores. In a few instances, "maids" waited on them. Their homes were "ridden" with "gadgets." The only available entertainment was "commercialized." Ken used a boy he called "Gerry Atkins" to demonstrate the harm that could occur. Gerry "was the product not only of suburbia but of a dismaying amount of parental indulgence. The good stuff that is within every youngster was in Gerry's case overlaid by indolence, by an inability to command the will to do anything unpleasant, demonstrated by a complete lack of inner discipline, an egocentric personality, a flabby body and a jaded mind. All at 12 years of age."[50]

What Gerry needed, Ken implied, was a program based on the ideals he and the back-to-the-landers had in common. Although historians disagree about the extent to which economic difficulty motivated people to flee cities at the turn of the twentieth century, they agree that all homesteaders have shared a commitment to simplicity, self-sufficiency, and hard work.[51] As we will see in the next chapter, the camps embodied all three: rugged accommodations, opportunities to learn self-reliance, and challenging work projects.

The Webbs shared with the back-to-the-landers not only a dedication to a set of values but also a belief in the sanctity of nature. As religion professor Rebecca Kneale Gould notes, "The practice of homesteading often involves religious or spiritualized visions of nature that have a long, dynamic history in American culture."[52] In *Summer Magic*, for example, Ken wrote,

> It is good for a boy or girl to stretch his ordinary frame of thought periodically, to be still a few moments and ponder on the universality of such laws as that of love, kindness, and consideration for others. . . . It is good for a youngster to reflect on the miracle of a mother rabbit tearing out tufts of her own fur to make a snug nest for her helpless pink babies, and to try to fathom the mystery of it all. . . .
>
> And it is well for a boy to ponder on the quiet of his own thoughts whence the glorious hues of sunset, the sheen of moonlit waters, the dainty bloom of some wild-ling of the woods. Whence come these colors, whence the delight of our response, whence the exultant joy of vigorous action—whence the depths when we listen in our own aloneness? . . .

These are all experiences which the rush and efficiency of modern urban life tend to crowd out. These are the precious opportunities of spiritual growth for which a camp can provide time and an ideal setting.[53]

In different words, Ken and Susan repeated these sentiments over and over.

KEN ALONE

On his own, Ken played a prominent role in the national camp movement. The head of the association of Vermont camp directors for many years, he was a highly visible presence at the meetings of the American Camp Association. In 1961, he edited *Light from a Thousand Campfires*, a collection of essays for the association, and was the major writer of "Camping for American Youth," a manuscript the publications committee planned to submit to various journals.[54]

Although the Webbs wrote within a long tradition when they touted the spiritual qualities of nature, one aspect of Ken's nature writing, his advocacy of nudism, may have shocked many of his readers. "We say we wish to live in communion with nature," he wrote in the *Thunderbird*, the Timberlake newspaper in 1970, "yet we insulate ourselves from nature (as if it were a hostile entity) by wearing too many clothes and wearing them when they are unnecessary."[55] Three years later, he casually described the origins of nudism at F&W in a story told many times but quite possibly apocryphal. He had been the director of a day camp near Buffalo, New York, in 1938 when he took a group of boys and another counselor to explore Vermont as a possible place to relocate. The one problem he found with what was otherwise a spot "ideally suited to a boys' camp" was the rain. Hiking along the Appalachian Trail to Stratton Pond, one boy suggested that the campers go barefoot to keep their shoes dry. Another demurred: that way they would have dry shoes to wear home but wet clothes. And still, another suggested hiking entirely bare. And so they did, starting a tradition, Ken wrote, that "Timberlake has ever since enjoyed, the Fifth Freedom, a freedom from clothes whenever no *rational* answer can be given to the question of why not?"[56]

But Ken's fascination with nudism probably had more complex roots than practicality on a rainy day. In the early 1930s, tourists and journalists impressed with the German nudism movement had introduced the practice in the United States. In the summer of 1936, two years before the hike to Stratton Pond, a nudist camp in Valparaiso, Indiana, had hosted the fifth Annual International Nudist Conference, celebrating the remarkable progress the movement had achieved in America and looking forward to greater growth and prosperity. American nudists, like the Germans they followed, downplayed the erotic aspects of the practice, touting instead the healing benefits of exposing the entire body to the sun, light, and air.[57] In a 1969 letter to the editor of the *Friends Journal*, Ken wrote, "Many of our parents, who are doctors, have approved enthusiastically this practice as a means of strengthening health and resistance to colds." Moreover, Ken insisted, nudism did not encourage immorality. "Only the so-called lower middle class," he continued, "still see a connection between nudity and sexual license."[58] Indeed, Ken appears to have viewed the absence of clothes, even in coed situations, as a bulwark against sexual desire.[59] Nudism, he declared, encouraged "wholesome attitudes."[60]

Perhaps because Ken wanted to reach the widest possible audience, his camp writing was largely apolitical. With the notable exceptions of railing against consumerism and encouraging racial integration in camps, these publications gave no indication that he endorsed progressive social change. Only in *As Sparks Fly Upward*, published in the midst of the Vietnam War protests, did he register his disapproval of the status quo. He condemned U.S. foreign policy, reprinted the letter he had sent to numerous draft boards on behalf of former campers and counselors applying for conscientious objector status, and expressed pride in those who participated in progressive social movements.[61] In the 1940s, 1950s, and early 1960s, however, he presented himself as adhering to the Cold War consensus.

Ken was far more forthright in his letters to the editor of the *Rutland Daily Herald*. An inveterate letter writer, he expressed his opinion on a wide range of issues. Some of these, too, were noncontroversial. He wrote about billboards and the color of poison ivy in the fall, in support of India, and against both legalized betting and dumping cars. In addition, he focused on topics related to the camps, such as motorboats on small lakes like Woodward Reservoir and a dispute about an island on Lake Ninevah. He also called attention to camp activities he thought would appeal to the public, such as the efforts campers made to clean up a cemetery, fight a local fire, and participate in environmental work.

But Ken also was courageous when he took positions on issues that could brand him a leftist at the time, particularly in Vermont, which was still deeply conservative. In 1947, he condemned discrimination against Jews. A Miss Judith Leventhal had made a reservation at Russell Inn, in Peru, Vermont. The owner replied that her inn was "restricted and judging from your name you are Jewish" and returned her check. Ken responded with a letter titled "Racial Discrimination" in *the Rutland Herald*: "For the ten years that we have run Camp Timberlake in Plymouth, Vermont," he wrote, "we have prized the friendship of a number of Jewish parents and have found that our other parents have welcomed the opportunity for their children to live democratically with fine people of other races." The following year, Ken censured universal military training. Throughout the 1950s, he wrote against Joe McCarthy and H-bomb tests and about the need for education rather than bombs to stop communism.

Ken's 1958 endorsement of Bill Meyer as a peace candidate for Congress generated considerable controversy. A forester and conservationist, Meyer took positions to the left of Democratic leaders in Vermont: he recognized Red China, advocated banning nuclear weapons testing, and supported an end to the military draft.[62] Ken's support for Meyer (in an advertisement) drew the attention and ire of Clifford B. Harwood, MD, of Manchester, especially after the Webbs' daughter Susan (Sukie) began to work in Meyer's DC office.[63] The enraged doctor chided Ken for getting his daughter a job and then directly asked Ken whether he favored "U.S. diplomatic recognition of Red China, and the admission of Red China to the United Nations?" In his response, Ken noted that his daughter had "left a good job as administrative assistant to the head of the National Planning Assn. in Washington in order to be in Meyer's office" and that her salary was lower in her new position. In addition, he argued that the ad that he had supported was unlikely to have "swung" the election. Most significantly, in response to the direct question, he "readily" answered, "I agree with Sen. Fulbright, chairman of the senate Foreign Relations Committee, who said 'while I do not believe that the United states should recognize Communist China at the present time in view of their continued belligeerence [sic] and offence matters, I do not believe it is wise to continue to ignore the over 500,000,000 people in the China mainland in the naïve belief that they will somehow go away.'"[64]

SUSAN'S COMMUNITY WORK

Perhaps because Susan had spent most of her life in Vermont, she was better equipped than Ken to engage in community activities. According to local newspapers, in the 1940s and 1950s, she was secretary of the Woodstock League of Women Voters, a member of the planning commission of the Woodstock Congregational Church, a representative from Woodstock to a recreation committee, hostess at a meeting of "The Friendly Circle," a teacher of the seventh grade Sunday school at the congregational church, a participant in a Red Cross drive, a speaker for the philanthropic organization the King's Daughters, and president of the Rutland Girls Scouts Association.[65] We assume Susan viewed these myriad activities not only as part of her civic duty but also as a way to smooth F&W's acceptance in the community.

Susan's work on behalf of integration also supported the camps. In 1947, the year Farm & Wilderness enrolled its first African American campers, the *Vermont Standard* noted that she attended a "study group which is considering interracial problems" and that she would give a talk to the group stressing "the achievements of Negroes." Subsequently, Susan worked on racial issues primarily through the Church Women United (CWU), a group bringing together women from various denominations. In 1961, the CWU announced a major plan of action designed to challenge "the vestiges of racism within the CWU movement, the church, and the larger society." That year, Susan used her family's eminent roots to write a letter to the *Rutland Daily Herald* criticizing the refusal of the Daughters of the American Revolution to allow Marian Anderson to sing and raise money for UNICEF. Signing the letter with her full name, Susan Howard Webb, she wrote,

> Growing up, as I did, in a family dedicated to the finest traditions of our country as it was represented by such organizations as the Sons of the American Revolution, Daughters of the American Revolution, Society of Colonial Wars, and the Loyal Legion, many of our activities were with the splendid people who belonged, men and women who knew history and were proud of our heritage. This background must be that of thousands of other American children. Their shock must be great, indeed, as was mine at learning that these women, Daughters of the American Revolution, can accept such actions as keeping Marion Anderson out of their concert hall and now urging members not to support UNICEF.[66]

Four years later, she wrote about Martin B. Duberman's "very excellent" play *In White America*. Noting that the play was "based on documents describing the life of the Negro in America," she commented that it left her "and many others with the need to right a wrong too long neglected." As evidence that other audience members "came away saddened and wiser," she wrote that "one friend, who had never taken Negro children in her very fine summer camp, said, 'Where can I find a fine Negro camper? I can't put this off any longer.'" Without boasting that her camp had already begun to include African American campers, Susan indicated that she had traveled through Alabama and Georgia, where she found that Black people "are looked down upon, are not given opportunities for education, good jobs, etc. [and] are living in the poor unkempt sections of cities and towns."[67]

Like Ken, Susan also publicly opposed the Vietnam War in the late 1960s. When the *Rutland Daily Herald* published the now famous photograph of a Vietnam woman prisoner with a U.S. Marine rifle at her temple, Susan commented that the picture should "shock every one of us into writing our Congressmen and our President and by every means insisting that the warfare and bombing be halted, and this conflict ended."[68] In 1968, she wrote a letter opposing Hubert Humphrey for president because he stood by Lyndon B. Johnson, although she also acknowledged people had no choice but to vote for him. The same year, she urged a declaration be sent to the People's Poll headquarters in Lexington, Massachusetts, saying that they voted for Humphrey but would ask him "to repudiate clearly Johnson's Vietnam policies" and would enclose twenty-five cents to defray the costs of publication of the poll. If any money were to be left over, Susan wrote, the money would be donated "to civil rights causes."[69]

After directing the camps for thirty-one years, Susan joined the Vermont legislature for four terms (eight years), running initially as a Republican and then on both parties' tickets. She counted among her achievements several actions designed to protect women and girls: a bill to allow women to borrow money from banks without a man's cosignature, a Comprehensive Health Education Bill for teenagers, and a bill preventing one parent from taking a child out of the country without the permission of the other.[70] An article titled "Defining Moments: An Examination of the Gender Divide in Women's Contribution to Outdoor Education" describes Susan as "a visionary outdoor educator ... [with] a long career dedicated to improving the lives of children and women and their access to the outdoors."[71] When she died in 2011, the Vermont state legislature honored her "for her lifelong service as an educator, public servant, and civic and religious leader."[72]

KEN AND SUSAN AS CAMP DIRECTORS

Everyone we interviewed acknowledged that although Ken and Susan shared many ideals, they also had different strengths and weaknesses. Whether consciously or not, Ken hired several staff who were sexual predators; several people told us that at one point, he also employed a photographer who had previously been jailed for indecent behavior to take pictures of the scantily clad or naked boys at Timberlake. He was driven by ambition, always determined to start new camps, and never relinquished the dream that at least one (e.g., Seaforth in the British Virgin Islands) would become a year-round venture with school in the winter and camping in the summer. Len Cadwallader, who became the business director shortly after Ken and Susan transferred the camps to the Farm & Wilderness Foundation, said Ken had "grandiose plans."[73] Some, like the conservation of land around Lake Ninevah, Cadwallader noted, were "wonderful." But trying to start a camp in the Caribbean brought the camps to a "critical breaking point."

Cadwallader agreed with many others that Susan was far more practical and, along with the accountant, tried to "put the brakes on Ken's aspirations." But Ken could easily circumvent financial advice: he would simply "sign papers before they had a chance to say no." In telling the story of her life, Susan drew the same contrast. She took on the responsibility for finances because Ken was "hopeless" in that realm. As for herself, Susan said she "loved running things."[74]

Like a few others with whom we spoke, Jane Wohl, a camper at Indian Brook in the early 1960s, remembered that Susan not only provided an important balance to Ken's impracticality but also was a strong leader who at times responded sensitively to the needs of her campers.[75] Because Wohl was on a campership, she was supposed to leave after the first month, but Susan took her aside and told her she could stay if she wanted because there was an "extra bed." Perhaps in light of this moment, Wohl characterized Susan as being both "gentle" and "kind." Helen Seitz, an IB camper a decade before Wohl, recalled that after a Virginia boarding school expelled her, Susan helped her gain admission to a Quaker one.[76] Yet another ex-camper lauded Susan for having recognized the unique needs of her sister who had characteristics that now would place her on the autism spectrum. The sister added that Susan had advised her not to go on to Tamarack Farm: "My mom tried to apply for me to go to the farm. And then Susan Webb said to my mom, 'Well, the farm is really not for her.' . . . And you know, when I think about it, I kind of realize she was right. The farm was coed. I was not able to really relate to boys. I could not, I mean, it was hard enough for me to relate to girls."[77] Those comments suggest that Susan knew her campers well and intervened when she found it necessary to do so. Peg Espinola, an IB camper in the 1940s, recounted an incident that demonstrated both characteristics. Because she had not been able to thwart the placement in her cabin of a friend from home whom she had outgrown, Espinola convinced the other girls in her cabin to be mean to the poor girl. Apparently, Susan learned about this behavior and "convened the girls [in the cabin] other than the victim and said, in effect, 'We hear you're doing really bad stuff and you have to stop.'"[78]

Our own memories and conversations with our peers reveal other aspects of Susan's personality and leadership. Ann Scattergood Fogg, who was a camper in the 1950s and then returned as an adult with a young child to work as a staff member, remembered that although Susan "was the force behind things," she was very "quiet . . . sort of in the background."[79] Unlike the directors Fogg subsequently worked under, Susan was unlikely to "go around and be with campers and talk to campers in the dining hall." Others added that Susan was censorious when she detected any kind of sexual activity and, as we show in chapter 4, quick to humiliate campers who transgressed her idea of moral behavior. (We also suggest in that chapter that this attitude might have provided protection for campers at IB.) Susan picked favorites and made occasionally hurtful pronouncements comparing the campers and counselors she valued with those she deemed less worthy. Some people have also described her as lacking a sense of humor, being irritated rather than amused at the practical jokes played by members of the staff.

The contrasts between the messages Ken and Susan wrote in the camps' newspapers highlight some of their differences. Ken's essays in the *Thunderbird* were less invitations than admonitions to behave and fulfill his notion of the model camper. The essays followed the contours of the summer schedule, beginning with a welcome to the campers, reminding them to participate in all the camps had to offer, exhorting them to cultivate the characteristics he considered ideal, celebrating the various festivities, and concluding with an assessment of achievements at the end of the summer. By contrast, Susan's messages to her campers in the *Lightning Bug* were brief—frequently less than half a page, double-spaced. Hers also followed the sequence of significant events: She welcomed campers at the beginning of the summer, urged them to take stock midway through the eight-week session, reminded them to assess their accomplishments toward the end of the summer, and celebrated the traditions of the bonfire on the Fourth of July and the fair. She supplemented this standard fare with frequent writings about natural beauty, the significance of chapel and the acquisition of skills, and the "'abiding assets' of health, friendliness, helpfulness, faith, hope and love, and consecration to use our talents and our skills well in order to best serve others."[80] Her homilies were less philosophical ruminations than invitations to be reflective, act generously, and "go the second mile."

Pretty much everyone we interviewed who was associated with the camps during Ken and Susan's leadership remembers one other key difference: while Ken walked around nude (and occasionally greeted parents wearing nothing but a watch and his orthopedic shoes), Susan rarely even ventured to the waterfront; when she did, she always wore a bathing suit.

2 · RUGGEDNESS

In the introduction, we asked whether Farm & Wilderness was unique. Certainly, we felt that way when we were there: that we were having some grand and unusual adventure. Other people went to camp; we went to F&W. Ken, more than Susan, created and then touted the mystique of uniqueness. In the Timberlake newspaper, the *Thunderbird* (which campers would have been more likely to read than his other writings), he periodically spelled out the special features of the camps, especially of his beloved Timberlake (TL). Two years after the camp opened, he wrote that he expected TL boys to cultivate certain qualities including friendliness, reliability, neatness, punctuality, being "always direct, frank, and straightforward," and cooperation. In 1945, he told a visitor that he had been "trying to create a type of living that would be clean and wholesome, self-reliant, simple, and unselfish. Now we know that our plans were good, and a certain ruggedness and straightforwardness is built into the very fabric of our life together."[1] Some of the ideal characteristics of TL boys—reliability, neatness, punctuality, and being "always direct, frank, and straightforward"—receded over time, to be replaced by different traits. Ruggedness, however, remained central. As an adjective, rugged became applied to many aspects of camp. In 1957, it described the hike that well-trained campers can "take in stride," leaving behind good memories. At other times, "rugged" was conjoined with Quaker simplicity.

Pondering what TL sought in its staff, Ken wrote in 1957 that he was interested in people with maturity and responsibility who could help mold the ideal TL boy. And that would be someone who, through "his experience here has strengthened his native integrity, maturity, responsibility, and who has a respect for rugged, simple living, who is able to find satisfaction in work, who enjoys wilderness living, who has a reverence for nature and a growing sensitivity to things of the spirit."[2] Simplicity, then, was not enough. Camp life also demanded endurance and toughness. A year later (1958), Ken repeated this phrase. Recounting the story of a father and son who went winter camping, he noted that as they settled in for the night, the father pushed away the block of ice the boy had opted to use as a pillow. Ken insisted that they did not have to go that far at TL "in following our ideal of rugged simplicity."[3]

Ken also allied ruggedness with health and his notion of the ideal body. If TL need not go as far as the father who refused the merest indulgence, it should not go too far in the other direction either. Astonishing to contemporary ears, Ken wrote that "we don't want to bring up any pansies here either." And he continued that after a few weeks at camp, the boys should be "toughening up." Later, in the same summer of 1958, he commented, "This is no place for cream-puffs," and that it is unlikely that the camp harbors any such individuals.[4] A year later, Ken's column lauded the "rugged satisfaction in a challenging work-out that tests both muscles and co-ordination" and expressed his hope that the summer has produced not only health but also "some degree of ruggedness."[5] Again, in 1962, Ken reminded campers that one of the most important things that TL offers but no other camp (except IB) does is "ruggedness."[6] The following year as well, he promulgated the standards and self-discipline that should go into making "one's body the rugged well-muscled, clean and efficient instrument it can be."[7]

By the 1970s, Ken had simplified his list of the unique qualities of the F&W camps. Now ruggedness was entirely distinct from simplicity: the latter meant paring down, being able to do without luxuries; the former meant something even more, a toughness and determination that enabled a boy to "hike all day and then have energy left to set up a good camp and perhaps play an active game in the evening."[8]

At TL, the rugged bodies were displayed as well as produced. There, boys swam and sometimes played sports in the nude. Some former campers remember what was called "the Fifth Freedom" as a great privilege. Others recall some uneasiness. One former camper put it this way: "I think in the beginning I was self-conscious about the nudity, and I wasn't that into it."[9] Others suggested that some coercion had been involved. A man who had been at Timberlake told us that Ken "was very pushy about it" and that "if an occasional camper at Timberlake really insisted on wearing his bathing suit, he was teased." Neither of us remembers "the Fifth Freedom" being a central issue at Indian Brook (IB) when we were there. We wore bathing suits for swimming lessons in the morning; we were allowed to shed them for free swim later in the day. Others might have felt more coercion and discomfort when they resisted. One former camper wrote about this practice: "I feel strongly that it was harmful to me. I was a child who could not show her body publicly, and the expectation of nudity left me the only one in a bathing suit, which was excruciating."[10]

As we explain in chapter 4, that changed when girls at IB insisted that they should be able to do everything that the boys did. At Tamarack Farm, in spite of Ken's assumption that nudism would forestall sexual curiosity and desire, skinny-dipping was even more exciting. But some campers from our time—and

FIGURE 3. Swimming dock near the dam. Photograph courtesy of Margaret Nelson.

even more so from later years when nudism became a more prominent feature of IB—remember the value of learning that bodies came in all different shapes and sizes. And many campers—men and women alike—bemoaned the elimination of the practice in 2007, believing that an especially valuable aspect of Farm & Wilderness had been lost.[11]

The outpost camps prided themselves on their special ruggedness. A camper at Saltash Mountain (SAM) in the first few years after it opened remembered it as "a very isolated place," where boys cooked at least two meals a day over an open fire. The idea was that "we're going to strip everything down to make it a very simple life, and you take care of yourself and take care of others." After 1969, when Flying Cloud's director Rick Hausman launched "The Great Leap Backward" (in contradistinction to Mao's Great Leap Forward), that camp represented an extreme version of F&W austerity. Rick Hausman explained to us that he wanted to teach a group of older boys that they could live independently on "a little patch of land in Vermont."[12] The campers produced as well as cooked all the food and gathered wood for fuel. The only refrigeration came from ice that had been cut during the winter. The radio that previously had connected SAM and Flying Cloud was turned off. Flashlights were forbidden. Vehicles could not come within a mile of the camp. As a result, Jane Wohl, a codirector with her

FIGURE 4. The oven at Flying Cloud. Photograph courtesy of Nate Hausman.

husband, Barry, after Rick Hausman, said, "All of our groceries were delivered to the gravel pit, and we would get our backpacks and go down to the gravel pit and bring the groceries up. . . . We had no matches. We lit the fire at the beginning of the summer [with a bow drill], and that fire stayed going all summer long."[13]

At Flying Cloud, as at Timberlake, ruggedness had a distinctly masculine flavor. The camp was for boys alone. Rick Hausman recalled, "We had lots of phony macho pride in being tougher and, you know, more rugged than anybody else." Nevertheless, ruggedness was a striking feature of F&W as a whole. Boys and girls alike, from the age of eight or nine, slept in crude accommodations, embarked on strenuous hiking and canoe trips, and engaged in hard physical labor.

ACCOMMODATIONS

Ken was not the only camp director to describe the post–World War II generation of children as pampered and coddled, but whereas many others sought to cater to children's sensitivities in their living arrangements, he wanted to foster hardiness and toughness. According to historian Abigail A. Van Slyck, advice manuals for camp directors in the 1940s "took for granted the necessity of

FIGURE 5. A cabin at Tamarack Farm, exposed to the elements. Photo courtesy of John Wilhelm.

providing electricity to the dining hall, infirmary, administration building, [and] the pump house . . . The pump house helped supply the ample water that was piped to the flushing toilets, hot showers, and drinking fountains."[14] Camp brochures displayed fully enclosed cabins with bathrooms and often special eating and recreation areas. By contrast, F&W campers continued to use out-houses (which they called KYBOs). The cabins lacked running water and were open to the air on at least one side. Surrounded only by trees, they exposed campers to the vagaries of the weather. Judy Polumbaum, a camper at Indian Brook in the 1970s, remembered living "deep in the woods." She elaborated, "You really felt this daily constant connection to nature for good or ill. I mean, sometimes it was freezing. Sometimes it rained. Sometimes it was too hot. There were mosquitoes."[15] Without electric lights, campers had to find their way in the dark on treacherous dirt paths. Cindy Amatniek was ten when she arrived at IB in 1968. "From the first night," she later wrote, "I remember step-ping out of the cabin into the darkness that seemed to go on forever. I felt like my foot might not touch the ground. This was very different from suburban NY."[16] Janine Fay, who started at IB in 1958 at age thirteen, remarked that liv-ing without modern conveniences was "exciting. You felt sort of on the edge going to a KYBO."[17] And she enjoyed living by nature's rhythms: "It was dark. That's it, go to bed."

CAMPING TRIPS

When Ken Webb wrote in a 1956 *Thunderbird* that Farm & Wilderness camps were known for having "the best hiking program in the East," he undoubtedly meant that the hiking and canoe trips were exceptionally long and strenuous and that, because all campers were adequately prepared, they could dispense with elaborate equipment.[18] Campcraft was thus a major activity. A series of ratings (Woodsman, Pioneer, and Pathfinder) indicated the skills campers had to master before joining more difficult hikes. Hoping to qualify as a campcraft counselor, Cathy Wilkerson, who first came to Indian Brook as a counselor's apprentice in 1961, "worked hard to learn all the required skills." Overcoming her fear of axes, she learned "how to cut down a tree, how to split wood, how to replace an axe handle and sharpen the blade." She learned about different kinds of knots and their purposes. And she learned "how to make shelters in the wild with ponchos, to dig trenches for drainage, to dig a latrine and a grease pit, to disassemble the campsite so no one could tell we have been there . . . and how to judge if stream water was safe to drink and how to purify it if need be."[19]

Peg Espinola, a camper at Indian Brook in the 1940s, recalled her delight in finally becoming proficient in a physical activity. She describes herself as a clumsy child who was terrible at jump rope, hopscotch, or any activity involving a ball.[20] At camp, she discovered that she had a lot of stamina and so was "great at hiking" and "great at canoeing." But some women we interviewed focused on the difficulties they encountered. "I found hiking hard," Carol Rapaport Monteleoni, an IB camper in the 1950s, commented. "I remember I had this way of self-talk. Like we'd be hiking up a hill and I would put my foot down and I would say to myself, okay, that step is a thing of the past."[21] Janine Fay liked canoe trips but hiking "not so much." She commented, "I didn't like doing that schlepping a big thing on my back and trudging on. No I didn't enjoy that."[22] And when we asked Helen Seitz, who had been at Indian Brook in 1950, how she felt about the hikes, she laughed and said, "We did the five-day hike to Mansfield, and I convinced everybody that we should take the chair lift up. Which we did."[23] She enjoyed being on the top, she said, but not climbing uphill.

Accounts by other women mirrored Ken's major theme: strenuous hiking and canoe trips taught campers that with enough willpower and determination, they could triumph over all adversity. In *Beyond Our Wildest Dreams*, the Webbs quoted Lisa Shamberg, an IB camper in 1958, who discovered the thrill of overcoming challenges on a canoe trip on the Connecticut River. "Well," she wrote in the *Lightning Bug*, "we're all back and still in good health, miraculous as it may seem after you hear about some of our experiences." Rain increased the difficulties of portages. Lightning forced the group to abort one trip through rapids. One evening, they found a dry place to stay "so things were all right again," but they then discovered that one canoe was missing. (After hunting for it for an hour, they found it in good shape a few miles away.) Shamberg concluded, "We all had a wonderful time and came back, sort of wishing we could have stayed six more days."[24]

Mindy Thompson Fullilove was another enthusiastic propagandist for F&W's camping trips. In her case, the lessons she learned remained with her throughout her life. She first came to Tamarack Farm as a babysitter when she was fourteen. As either a "respite or reward," she was allowed to join a weeklong mountain hike. Unfortunately, she lacked proper equipment: "I borrowed some hiking boots that didn't fit, an ancient backpack that distributed weight so as to increase the poundage, and a threadbare sleeping bag." By the third mountain, she realized she "was in agony." She explained, "I was astounded at how steep those old mountains were and how hard and cold they could be. But it was the fact that there was one mountain after another that did me in." She "stood at the top of that awful rock and all I could see in any direction was wild, steep mountain." With no alternative, she persevered. As she continued to climb, "things got worse; the ill-fitting boots raised a massive blister on my heel. I shivered all through the nights in the threadbare sleeping bag. My shoulders ached from the pack I had to lug." Finally, she slid down the final mountain to the van that would take her back to camp. But she never forgot that moment when she saw that endless row of mountains she had to cross. "I learned on that trip that

FIGURE 6. Campers on a hike. Photo courtesy of John Wilhelm.

my body could make it," she wrote. "I learned something about faith in others. I learned a lot about the darkest hour that comes just before the dawn."[25]

Years later, she decided that the best gift she could give her daughter Molly was to offer her the same opportunity, to teach her that she, too, could overcome adversity. As a camper at Saltash Mountain Camp, Molly went on a combined canoeing and hiking trip to Flagstaff, Maine. "The hiking was every bit as hard as she had thought it would be but not harder than what she could manage," Fullilove wrote. "Her joy as she reached the top was overwhelming. She nearly ran to the top, just to be there." When Molly returned, she wrote to her parents, "I know now, that when things get hard, I'll remember that I did Flagstaff."[26]

Although accounts in the Timberlake *Thunderbird* also tended to glorify the hardships campers experienced on the trail, the men we interviewed said little about them. Asked what was most important to him about Timberlake, David Finkelhor, a camper in the late 1950s, replied that he associated it with "[his] love of the outdoors and the kind of outdoor skills that [he had learned]." He added, "I learned all the campcraft skills. I learned about hiking. I have wonderful memories about the hikes and the canoe trips I took and all the places in New England that I explored in those times."[27] Barry Wohl, whose first year at TL was in 1957 and who subsequently became both a counselor and director at Flying Cloud, developed a passion that remained with him throughout his life.[28] He took his first trip when he was in the youngest cabin. Because it was a training hike, each camper built his own poncho tent. When it started pouring, the two counselors built a large fire and decided to sleep in the lean-to shelter. "The rest of us," he recalled, "started out in poncho shelters, and I remember about eleven or twelve at night, one counselor brought me a piece of soggy strawberry shortcake and asked if I wanted to come into the shelter with the other boys, and I said, 'No, I'll stay here.' So I spent the whole night in the poncho tent, and my sleeping bag was half soaked, and I was shivering, but it changed my life forever, really that night." Years later, Barry told us, he moved to Wyoming "because [he] fell in love with the wilderness at F&W." Now in his seventies, he continues to rely on skills acquired at camp as he tests himself against the elements: "Yesterday I went with my best friend up in our mountains here. We didn't see anyone for five hours, and I never would've done that if Farm & Wilderness hadn't introduced me to backpacking when I was ten years old. . . . Living all those summers in an Indian tepee and cooking over open fire and getting lost, it just doesn't bother me to be walking out in the woods and getting lost." Trips like these, Barry added, helped him relieve the tensions of working as a solo-practitioner: "My career as a pediatrician was so wonderful, but so stressful. Every day, you had the potential to hurt somebody by making wrong decisions. . . . But when I would go hiking in the mountains around Sheridan and where I am now . . . I knew I'd find peace."

Some men said that their love of the outdoors, which began at Farm & Wilderness, served as a bond with others. Neil Rolnick, who spent his first summer at TL in 1957 as a young boy and later moved on to Tamarack Farm, commented that he has "a bunch of friends" from camp "who are really close, who had been with me all these years. And the people I knew at camp are the people that are still interested in going and climbing mountains with me and going on long, long walks and doing things outdoors."[29] Our brothers, Jimmy and Tom Klein, still hike together whenever they can (at least once a year), and Tom spends weeks in the summer in the Italian Alps with his wife. Forty years ago, Jimmy and Tom taught Emily's husband, Rick, what they had learned at Timberlake, and every year since then, he has backpacked in the Sierras one week in the spring and another in the summer. Over sixty years after he spent a few summers at Timberlake, Peggy's husband, Bill, found his happiest moments climbing one of the peaks in Vermont's Green Mountains.

WORK PROJECTS

Other camps might have required that campers do chores. In Laurie Kahn's book of reminiscences, *Sleepaway*, Bernice Haase Luck, who attended Camp Beverly between 1942 and 1945, wrote that although at home she had "no chores," at camp, she "learned about a personal discipline, a sense of self, and that there were ways of doing things other than my family's style." Over time, she added, she came to like "not feeling lazy" and "being neat." Another camper at a Girl Scouts camp expressed less enthusiasm, at least for the job of cleaning the john; her favorite activity on the "chore wheel" was sweeping.[30]

Farm & Wilderness campers also did chores. We made our beds, cleaned our cabins, and set and cleared tables. These were routine, boring, and necessary. But our obligations extended far beyond "mere" chores. Each camper participated—whether willingly or not—in work projects: gardening, maintenance, construction, and caring for farm animals. Because the outpost camps were designed to foster independence, they placed a special emphasis on work projects. A 1968 issue of the *Lightning Bug* included a report from the campers at the short-lived Ko-Ko-Pah on Indian Lake in the Adirondacks. It carefully itemized the demands placed on the girls there: "After breakfast the fun, I mean work begins. We have all sorts of thrilling, exciting, and daring projects to do. Anyone want to come down to the waterfront and help remove all the wood from the water? How about making a path, or building a dishwashing area? Would you like to build a shelter for firewood, or over the cooking area?"[31] The following year, the wilderness outpost moved to an area closer to the original camps and was renamed Dark Meadow.

The Senior Work Camp (subsequently called Tamarack Farm [TF]) elevated work to the central activity. Helen Seitz might have been reluctant to climb uphill, but she had "no problem" doing the work required at what was then called, simply, the Farm. She remembered in particular that they worked on improving the drainage on the road and that the girls felt "very brave" stripping down to their bras. A *SEWOCA*, the TF newspaper, from the following year (1952) suggests that Helen's attitude might not have been shared by all campers and that some questioned the "value of the work done at Tamarack Farm." Campers, the author (identified only with the initials "P. L.") wrote, perceived a conflict between the work that would contribute to the Webbs' long-range vision for "a school-farm-camp complex in the valley" and the work required to allow the camp to "function properly." P. L. argued that the only activity that satisfied both was forestry: "Here we feel the satisfaction of physical exertion and the feeling of accomplishment when an area has been successfully treated with civil cultural techniques. At the same time it beautifies the area and prepares productive timber which helps fulfill the future plans of the camps."[32] A *SEWOCA* article from a decade and a half later (1968) indicated that campers continued to struggle with attitudes toward work projects. "Some of the camp," Dave Kuhn wrote, "has this year never gotten beyond the point of considering work only a chore; to be avoided if possible and gotten through with least effort if not."[33]

FIGURE 7. Campers putting a roof on a building at Tamarack Farm. Photo courtesy of John Wilhelm.

As we will see in chapter 4, physical labor had special meaning to Indian Brook girls in the 1970s who learned to trust their own bodies and dispense with male assistance. Other former campers from years earlier told us that the skills they acquired at F&W served them well throughout their lives. Susan Fletcher, who started at IB in 1955 at the age of ten, had often gone to her grandparents' farm, where her "grandmother had a huge garden." She remarked, "I was very eager to learn gardening so I could help her in the garden. I loved pasture clearance, which is something I do to this day up at the farm and love."[34] Nevertheless, many people remembered work projects as their least favorite camp activity. "We had to build things and fix things," Ann Scattergood Fogg, who started as an IB camper in 1952, said. "I didn't at that time, particularly like that part."[35]

CONCLUSION

The ruggedness of daily life at F&W helped us feel we had been transported to an entirely new place, where old rules no longer applied. Embracing the romanticism of living with nature and the allure of simplicity, we had tested our bodies in new ways. Sleeping in open-air cabins, embarking on rigorous hikes, and performing hard physical labor at Farm & Wilderness, we became different people, with new identities, feelings, and social relationships. Ruggedness also conferred a sense of superiority. At camp, we learned the expression "gotrocks," which, according to the online Oxford Reference, is "a facetious surname applied in US slang to a person of unseemly wealth."[36] At F&W, that phrase (written often as "gotrox") had transmuted into a general sneer directed at anyone or any activity less pure, less rigorous, less uncomfortable than those to which we were exposed to at camp. Mosquito nets? Gotrox. Freeze-dried food on hiking trips? Gotrox. Real tents? Gotrox. After Lisa Shamberg confessed that she and other members of her canoe trip spent one night in a shelter, she exclaimed, "What gotrox!" Although Cathy Wilkerson did not use the term "gotrox," she acknowledged displaying similar arrogance. After mastering the art of lighting "a one-match fire in the rain, using only material [she] could find in the woods," she acquired "contempt for non-woodsmen who had to use paper to start a fire."[37] At TL, the sense of exceptionalism often had a decidedly misogynist cast as at least some staff members insisted TL boys were tougher than not only other boys but also the girls at Indian Brook. A drawing in a 1952 *Thunderbird* was titled "The Arrival." On one side was a thin, sickly looking boy at "Camp Gotrox," dressed in a suit complete with a vest, top hat, and tie. He had a large suitcase as well as an umbrella and tennis racket. On the other side was a large, muscular boy at Camp Timberlake wearing only a bathing suit and carrying a small backpack. Only years later did we recognize that that smugness about living with so

FIGURE 8. Gotrox cartoon, from *Thunderbird*, an F&W publication.

few material possessions rested on an immense amount of strategic planning and invisible work.

At the end of the 1963 session, Tamarack Farm director Norm Williams wrote that he hoped most of the campers "acquired a new respect for hard physical work—for the skill, intelligence, and perseverance demanded by a workman-like job. Some might even feel that they have joined the great brotherhood of this world's builders and makers of things we have used daily without a thought. To gaze at a bridge or a skyscraper now and wonder how it was put together may be one result of having helped erect the woodshed and new boys' cabin."[38] If we had a new understanding of the dignity of physical work, however, most of us hoped to enter high-level occupations after attending elite colleges. Nevertheless, the way of life we had experienced at Farm & Wilderness exerted a pull. Although its simplicity may have been staged and temporary, it provided an ideal to which many campers continued to aspire long after they left.

We interviewed a few former campers and staff members who continued to live according to the values they had practiced at F&W. Paul Stone had played many roles at the camps over a long period of time, including building much of Seaforth, accompanied by his wife, Frances, and their four children. The Stones left in 1976 to start their own dairy farm. Subsequently, they shifted to raising turkeys in a large family operation in Orwell, Vermont. The Stones live in the log house Paul built, and even at eighty, Paul engages in hard physical labor. When Peggy called to arrange an interview for a Saturday afternoon, Paul said she should check first. If it were good weather and he hadn't yet finished with the lower field, he would be out haying. Topher and Marie Waring, another couple with a long association with F&W, lived pretty much "off the grid"—without wires, pipes, or cables—for a number of years in the Northeast Kingdom of Vermont, an area that remains scarcely populated even today. Although the idea of simplicity remained an aspiration for many of us following our summers at F&W, most had resumed familiar patterns after returning to homes filled with all the "gadgets" Ken deplored.

3 · "CAMPING FROM THE NECK UP"

In *Beyond Our Wildest Dreams*, the Webbs wrote, "A good friend of the camps, himself a camp director, invented the phrase, 'Camping from the neck up' to indicate that the activities of the long summer should not be aimed at the physical aspects of life only. We agreed."[1] Folk music, progressive politics, Quaker spirituality, and friendships were all major ingredients of a Farm & Wilderness summer.

MUSIC

The former Timberlake campers we interviewed highlighted the music program created and led by Jack Sloanaker for many years. The revelation in the early 1990s that Sloanaker had been a sexual predator throughout much of his long F&W career irredeemably damaged his reputation. Nevertheless, many men hoped we would not portray him simply as an abuser. The string bands he founded were legendary, playing at square dances and even producing two LP records. He also mentored generations of campers. One said, "The music program was very important to me. A lot of it was Sloanaker. I learned so much from that guy. He was a fountain of information. But there were other music people around, too."[2]

Some Timberlake alumni had celebrated music careers. We learned about Tony Parkes's Timberlake experience from interviews that had been conducted with him before we began our study. Now an internationally known producer, pianist, and square dance caller, Parkes remarked that he must have been destined to be a caller because he was at the "right place at the right time on so many occasions." His private elementary school "had a serious folk music and dance program that everybody was involved in. It wasn't an elective. You just did it." Nevertheless, he continued, "What really turned me on to it was the second summer that I went to the Farm and Wilderness camps in Vermont." Lying in his bunk as a ten-year-old and listening to the callers at night remained vivid in Parkes's memory: "I could usually tell you who was calling and what he was calling even that far away. So that was really exciting. And that was when I got hooked for life on the whole phenomenon of called dances." The summer he was twelve, Parkes was invited to play the piano with Sloanaker's band at square dances. "I had had some piano lessons, classical, and never really stuck with it. But I knew how to pound out the rhythm, oompah, oompah or boom-chuck, boom-chuck." The work was arduous: "There would be I think five square dances a week at the camps for the different age groups, and then one after hours for the staff." Parkes noted that Sloanaker "was the driving force behind the square dance program," but others also had an impact: "What I like to say these days is I saw 100 kids on the floor all doing the same thing at the same time because [the caller] said so, and I said, I want to be him. I didn't quite put it in those words, at age 10, 12, 14. But that's how I felt inside, that this was something I wanted to be part of, the three-way interaction between the caller and the musicians and the dancers. It was like magic."

When Parkes was fourteen, a member of Sloanaker's band asked if he was ready to call one of the dances the following night: "I said, 'Gulp, I am.' He had his eye on me, he saw me kind of mouthing along with him on the floor. He knew I was interested, he knew that this whole thing turned me on. . . . I got out there and my voice cracked three times. I think I remembered all the words in the right order. . . . So that went okay and a week or two later he had me call my first patter song." After six summers as a camper, Parkes returned one more year as a junior counselor and assistant caller. Although the musicians playing with Sloanaker undoubtedly considered Parkes exceptionally gifted and dedicated, he stressed that his experience was not unique: "A lot of other callers and musicians can point to Farm and Wilderness as one of the sources of their interest."[3]

Parkes later moved from New York to Boston "because a lot of people from Farm and Wilderness were in Boston during the winter. Either they went to Harvard, or they had been to Harvard or they wanted people to think they went to Harvard. There was a lot of crossover between Farm and Wilderness camps and the Boston, Cambridge, music scene." He may have met Neil Rolnick there. Rolnick is a composer whose music has been performed internationally; he is the recipient of numerous grants and awards. Between 1981 and 2013, he was a professor of music at Rensselaer Polytechnic Institute.[4] As a Timberlake camper, he, too, came under Sloanaker's tutelage. While a Harvard undergraduate, he joined a string dance band Sloanaker recommended and "ended up hanging out with a bunch of people who did various kinds of folk music all around the Northeast." When asked how his musical experiences at both Timberlake and Harvard had influenced his later career, he noted that although his compositions were "mostly classical and experimental," he often incorporated "folk tunes."

FIGURE 9. Campers playing music on the lawn at Tamarack Farm. Photo courtesy of John Wilhelm.

POLITICS

In addition to music, former campers and staff we interviewed from the 1950s and 1960s remembered Farm & Wilderness as a place where left-wing politics prevailed. Although F&W did not belong to the small group of self-proclaimed Communist camps, it shared many characteristics with them. It was interracial at a time when few White camps admitted African Americans. It served the same constituency, enrolling many children (including Tony Parkes) who attended Little Red School House and Elisabeth Irwin High School, two feeder schools to the Communist camps. It offered a refuge for children whose parents had been targeted by the Red Scare of the 1950s. And although Timberlake alone boasted a special music program, all of us who attended any F&W camp during the folk revival of the late 1950s and 1960s spent many hours listening to and performing folk music.

Because folk songs are now part of the standard repertoire of school choirs and popular singers, it may be important to explain the meaning the music had in the post–World War II era. "It is hard to exaggerate," wrote the *Broadside of Boston*, a folk music magazine, "how radically different" that music was "from the societal norms of the 1950s, and, in consequence how incredibly attractive it was. Years of study at high school and university were no match for the magnetic pull of musical electives like African-based work songs, medieval ballads, Delta blues, Appalachian songs, sea chanties, bluegrass, and dozens of other strains of American traditional music."[5] Robert Cantwell, an American Studies scholar, reminds us that the most famous musicians of the folk revival of the late 1950s and 1960s were not "the People" but rather members of a privileged segment of society. "However painstakingly authentic, however technically accomplished, however rare and antiquated their aural sources," he wrote, the folk singers of the era "were still mostly interpreters of folksong, not indigenous tradition bearers." Moreover, they did not invariably convey a particular ideology or promote an explicit political agenda.[6] Nevertheless, singing about the past struggles of marginalized groups and about the need to end war and racism gave many of us a vision of a better society we could carry with us after the summer ended.

Unlike Tony Parkes, who already was familiar with folk music when he arrived at Timberlake, some former campers told us that they first heard folk music at F&W and that the music helped introduce them to radical politics. John Wilhelm became a community organizer in the 1960s and later was president of the union UNITE HERE. He attended Tamarack Farm with Peggy in 1960 and spoke directly to her in his interview: "All of you introduced me to things. I just didn't know anything about folk music and the fact that there actually is such a thing as what we would call progressive politics that was broader than one person like my mother trying to do what she could on integration."[7] Cathy Wilkerson, who arrived at Indian Brook as a counselor's apprentice in 1961, later joined Students for a Democratic Society (SDS) and then the Weather Underground. She, too, attributed her political awakening in large part to the music she heard at F&W. A pivotal moment occurred when a girl put on a record in an old cabin that served as the camp's recreation center: "I had never heard folk music before. Miriam Makeba, Odetta, and the other performer sang about the injustice in the world, and about the efforts of ordinary people to survive. The passion of the music, about the brave, sometimes funny and sometimes tragic efforts of people to change the world, grabbed me by the heartstrings. During that summer of 1961, I heard the music of Josh White, The Weavers, Woody Guthrie, Pete Seeger, Peggy Seeger, Harry Belafonte, Flatt and Scruggs, Johnny Cash and Bill Watson."[8]

Some of the singers Wilkerson named were identified with left-wing politics. Woody Guthrie, often known as the father of modern American folk music, explained how his songs and politics were intertwined: "I think real folk stuff scares most of the boys around Washington. A folk song is about what's wrong and how to fix it, or it could be who's hungry and where their mouth is, and who's out of work and where the job is or who's broke and where the money is or who's carrying a gun and where the peace is—that's folk lore and folks made it up because they've seen that the politicians couldn't find nothing to fix or nobody to feed or give a job of work."[9] Although it is unclear whether he ever joined the Communist Party, he frequently played at Communist rallies. A sticker on his guitar read, "This Machine Kills Fascists." The original version of his most famous song, "This Land Is Your Land," written as a protest against Irving Berlin's "God Bless America," contained two verses condemning capitalism.[10]

Guthrie had a major influence on Pete Seeger, a central figure in the folk music revival, a mentor to many younger singers, and the writer of countless songs we sang at F&W. The first of his numerous albums, "Talking Union" was a mainstay of the American labor movement. Civil rights workers sang his adaptation of "We Shall Overcome" from an old spiritual. Other songs became rallying cries of the antiwar and environmental movements. Seeger was a member of several folk song groups, including the Weavers, which enjoyed enormous success after its founding in 1949 but disbanded following an investigation by the Senate Internal Security Subcommittee two years later. Seeger himself was subpoenaed by the House Un-American Activities Committee in 1955. Indicted in 1957 on ten counts of contempt of Congress, he was convicted in 1961 and sentenced to a year in prison. Although an appeals court dismissed the indictment, the John Birch Society and other right-wing groups picketed his concerts. "All those protests did was sell tickets and get me free publicity," he later remarked. "The more they protested, the bigger the audiences became."[11]

Many of the songs of Odetta and Miriam Makeba that Wilkerson heard in the Indian Brook recreation room similarly conveyed political themes. Called the "Voice of the Civil Rights Movement," Odetta described her training in classical music and musical theater at Los Angeles City College as "a nice exercise" but one that "had nothing to do with my life. . . . The folk songs were the anger." She marched with Martin Luther King Jr. and then sang "Oh Freedom" at the 1963 March on Washington. When Rosa Parks was asked which songs were most important to her, she replied, "All the songs Odetta sings."[12] Miriam Makeba was a South African singer who settled in the United States in 1959. Because many of her songs were critical of apartheid, the South African government denied her reentry into the country. Three years later, it banned her records and revoked her passport.[13]

Folk music was only one of the ways Farm & Wilderness transmitted and reinforced political messages. Weekly current events sessions were another. The existing *Thunderbirds*, *SEWOCAs*, and *Lightning Bugs* noted the topics discussed. These changed with the times. In the 1950s, campers debated such issues as "whether or not there should be Socialized Medicine in this country" and participated in discussions on the Far and Middle East (including the crisis in the Suez Canal). One evening, according to a *Lightning Bug* reporter, "Ken came up with a great surprise. This was a record called 'The Investigators,' a take-off on McCarthy and his investigations." During the 1960s, current events evenings included "information about the Poor People's Campaign," a debate on whether the voting age should be lowered to eighteen, a counselor's "acquaintance with the Black Muslims," a film on migrant labor (the "Harvest of Shame"), civil rights, Vietnam, soul music, poverty in American cities, and the CBS documentary on hunger. Following one meeting, a camper commented in the *Lightning Bug* that she had become aware of many events, including that the administration had asked "Congress to abolish the death penalty for all Federal crimes," that "a London court ordered James Earl Ray returned to the U.S. to stand trial," and that "eight people in chains staged a draft protest." The camper concluded, "Because of the many things that have happened in such a short time it is obvious how important and necessary Current Events is." Cindy Amatniek was a ten-year-old Indian Brook camper in 1968. "Was there ever another time during which current events were discussed that intensely?" she later asked before answering affirmatively, adding that "Susan brought in a small black and white TV for the moonwalk."[14] Other current events programs that summer explored student uprisings at colleges and universities.

Current events programming continued through the 1970s. A review of the summer's current events program in a 1976 *Thunderbird* reported that "more people came" each Monday night and that on the last evening, those involved "celebrated by going over to Ken Webb's house at Brooksend and watching the roll call for the Republican nomination for President."[15] In addition to scheduled events, the *Thunderbird* regularly reported on "non-camp news." An article on July 16, 1977, gave the history of the United Farm Workers; an editorial in the same issue urged campers to boycott grapes, head lettuce, and Gallo wines.

Throughout the years, current events evenings drew on staff who could offer special insights into the issue of race. One night, in 1956, head counselor Vera Chandler Foster (a social worker and wife of the president of Tuskegee University from 1953 to 1981) talked about segregation in the South; two decades later, Mabel Hicks, an African American cook at IB, spoke to the girls about her experiences in Birmingham, Alabama, and Nash Basom, a White counselor at Timberlake, presented his experiences working with the revolutionaries in a province in Africa. Periodically, foreign counselors gave reports about their countries (e.g., Ethiopia) or weighed in on a particular topic (e.g., two Egyptians spoke about their perspective on the Suez Canal).

Years later, campers could still remember the details of special programs. Berl Nussbaum, a camper at TL in the 1950s, told us about the evening "Ken brought in a speaker who [might have been Lebanese] and we just happened to hear a different perspective on the Middle East."[16] Nussbaum believed that "it was very unusual in a summer camp to have something like that happen." Cathy Wilkerson recalled, "[The] couple of times [when] we were visited by people who had been working in the civil rights movement in the South . . . I was impressed by these white people who defined their activism as a natural outcome of their belief in equality and their love of humanity."[17]

Political acculturation occurred in yet other ways as well. Some people we interviewed remembered that the parents of other campers served as role models for political activity. Even as a young camper at Indian Brook in the mid-1950s, Carol Rapaport Monteleoni was aware that Farm & Wilderness included "a lot of kids . . . whose parents were being persecuted one way or another in the McCarthy era," as well as "campers whose parents were civil rights activists in the South."[18] And many former campers remembered that informal conversations often centered on politics. Although Wilkerson had hoped to fall in love during her summer at F&W, she "was glad to meet young men who cared about the issues of poverty, civil rights, and peace, and who felt comfortable talking in a group, without the need to pair off."[19]

The left-wing politics that pervaded Farm & Wilderness in the 1950s and 1960s affected campers and staff in various ways. Barry Wohl, who spent many years as a camper at TL and eventually became a director at Flying Cloud, credited the camps with introducing him to ideas he soon adopted as his own.[20] He remembered being struck by the button against the House Un-American Activities Committee (HUAC) his Timberlake counselor wore because "I had never even heard of HUAC." After the 1963 session as a counselor's apprentice at Timberlake, he went with a few other campers and counselors to the March on Washington, "and it felt like extending the camp experience." Despite his father's disapproval, he protested the Vietnam War "all because of Farm & Wilderness." In a letter to Peggy, Jon Jacques described his experiences at TF in 1960 and 1961:

> A white bread kid from the heartland in Ohio. I had no clue about how the world outside really worked. My arrival at TF was filled with wonder as I was thrown into a mix of very bright and much better educated kids. It was life changing in that from that point onwards I tended to challenge authority even in the US Navy as my life unfolded there. My view of the Vietnam War was forged in being there and realizing the futility of our very unfortunate war of choice. I am grateful to all of my friends at Tamarack Farm. My life was changed by you all for the better.[21]

Like Wilkerson and Wilhelm, Janine Fay, who first came to IB in 1958, learned she could become not just political but also an activist for progressive causes.[22] Other former campers told us that they believe their parents chose Farm & Wilderness because they knew that their family values aligned with those of the camp. Monteleoni described her parents as having progressive values: "My father was a physician [who] was very, very opposed to fee for service medicine. He really believed that healthcare was a human right. Ultimately he worked for the auto workers union, where they had a prepaid medical plan that was about as close as you could get to a different delivery method. . . . And my mother was very politically involved with the League of Women Voters, the Urban League, and just always doing stuff." Monteleoni believed that her parents "very much felt like they were sending [my brother and me] there to get some good values. They had those values too. . . . So they were totally in sync with the kind of political orientation at F&W." Nick Thorkelson's first year at F&W was at Tamarack Farm in 1960. He thought that in sending him there, his parents were not just seeking alignment but also ensuring he did not stray too far from the fold: "I think summer camps are the means by which parents socialize their children into their secret tribes, whatever those may be. . . . I think my parents were alarmed that I was hanging out with a bunch of Republican farmers in Manchester, Connecticut, and they . . . heard all these nice things about Farm & Wilderness and they said, let's send him there. And . . . that'll keep him in our tribe."[23]

Still, other interviewees said that regardless of the reason their parents sent them to Farm & Wilderness, it reinforced the political beliefs they already had. One camper commented that the values he brought from home "were crystallized at camp."[24] Joan Countryman, who first came to Indian Brook in the 1950s, remembered expressing the political beliefs she had absorbed from her parents: "I brought them into the camps and nobody ever challenged them. They were stimulated but not rejected in any way."[25]

Because so many children of people who were radicals in the 1940s and 1950s joined protest movements in the 1960s and 1970s, it is difficult to estimate the extent to which summers at Farm & Wilderness were transformative. After telling us that he had attended the 1963 March on Washington with a friend, Neil Rolnick, who first went to TL in 1957 and continued to attend camp until 1963, noted that he could not "distinguish between the influence of the camp and the influence of my parents."[26] However, Berl Nussbaum, who was a little older than Neil when he first came to TL in 1958, remarked that although he arrived at the camps with progressive politics, his experiences there made him consider applying for conscientious objector status in the Vietnam War. (He ultimately decided he could not fulfill the legal requirements because he could not state unequivocally that he never would kill someone.)

Others used the bonds forged at camp to facilitate entry into specific organizations. After describing the years he spent in New Haven and Newark working on social movements in which former F&W campers were involved, Thorkelson stated that "camp landed me where I am now in new England [and] the whole world of community organizing and radical politics that I've participated in since [camp]." Similarly, Wilhelm said,

I owe a tremendous amount to Joan Cannady Countryman. When I transferred from Earlham to Yale in the fall of 1964, Joan and her then-husband, Peter Countryman, were in New Haven, both in graduate school. I looked her up, and she told me about a group of people who were interested in starting a community organizing project in the Hill neighborhood, a working class and poor mixed Italian, Black, and Puerto Rican area that had become a refuge (or a dumping ground, some would say) for people displaced by New Haven's urban renewal program. I got involved with that project, and it led to my life's work.

SPIRITUALITY

Because we remember Farm & Wilderness primarily as camps that fostered progressive political activity, we were surprised by the many people we interviewed who described them as deeply spiritual places. Ken and Susan Webb would have been pleased. "It is in the realm of a child's spiritual potential that camps can make their greatest contribution," Ken wrote in 1961.[27] Viewing nature as a sacred realm, the Webbs assumed that spiritual growth could occur as a matter of course at F&W throughout the day. Morning meetings for worship, known as "chapel" in the early years, crystallized the experience. Most were held outside. On Sundays, an entire camp (and sometimes several camps) met together for an hour-long session. On other mornings, smaller groups organized the meetings, which typically lasted fifteen minutes. Both types invariably included some singing as well as a talk by counselors or a director. Steve Curwood, a camper at TL in the 1950s and the current host of NPR's "Living on Earth," remembered Ken "teaching from Paul's second letter to the Corinthians and things like that."[28] Curwood added that in retrospect, he found it interesting that Ken "was not afraid of going to the Bible, and not afraid of going to the Gospels, despite how Jewish [the camp] population was." Occasionally, campers spoke. But the silence always constituted the main feature. Susan wrote to her campers, "Sitting in quiet meditation together helps us to feel closer, more helpful to each other and more loving. If we can leave our meetings with a renewed sense of loving kindness and thoughts of helping each other and determination to learn new skills and improve on old ones, each day will be more worthwhile for every camper."[29] Ken had more exalted expectations. He, too, wanted campers to ponder "the universality of such laws as that of love, of kindness, of consideration for others." In addition, they should "enlarge their sense of awe and wonder, gain a sense of wholeness, and realize they are part of something larger than themselves."[30]

Those ideals initially had little impact on young campers. Carol Rapaport Monteleoni recalled "giggling" with a friend and "pulling out grass and counting petals and kind of hunkering down in my sweatshirt."[31] In 2012, Cindy Amatniek wrote that she was busy the summer of 1968 "searching for 4-leaf clovers in the meeting circle by the Upper Lodge during Sunday Silent meeting. 45 minutes felt like forever to this 10 year old."[32] As the summer went on, however, many attitudes shifted. Judy Polumbaum, a counselor at IB in the early 1970s, was able to observe the change.[33] "I found it really interesting to watch how the kids, particularly kids who are new to this came to like it," she told us. "At first they were all antsy and would get up and talk sort of spout things off. And then by the end of the summer, it was this sacred space where everybody would shut up and people really took it seriously. And I just thought it was wonderful. I really did."

Various aspects of the meetings appealed to different campers. Barry Wohl focused on Ken's stories. He reminded us of the parable about the difference between heaven and hell: in hell, "everybody was sitting around long banquet tables, filled with the best food in the world and the best beverages. And everybody had long spoons tied from their wrist to their elbow. And so they were all starving. . . . [In heaven] it was the same picture, but everybody was feeding the person next to them." He then asked, "How can you forget that?" (Wohl now considers himself as "an atheist with stories.") For John Bancroft, "as a little kid at Timberlake, it was the quietness."[34] He also reveled in the beauty around him. "Sometimes we'd have a joint meeting with Indian Brook and Timberlake in a meadow," he recalled. "You're overlooking the horse barns and then the lake. It was the most gorgeous place in the world. Very inspiring." Ann Scattergood Fogg spent years at IB as a child and returned as an adult to be a staff member. Although she had been raised a Quaker and had attended a Quaker school, she said, "When I think of Quakerism, what I think of is sitting out in nature and looking at something really beautiful and being among people I really liked. . . . I can't imagine that at least sitting out there and looking at all this natural beauty didn't do something for people."[35]

A few alumni described a deeper sense of communion with nature. Cathy Wilkerson wrote, "One Sunday morning I sat on the grass with other counselors-in-training, in a huge circle on the lawn by the main lodge at the girls' camp. The only sound was the slight breeze softly rustling the thick foliage around the clearing. I felt the heat rising from the thick meadow grasses, enveloping me as I looked up at the clouds passing lazily across the sky."[36] Meetings on the dock could provide a sense of spaciousness. "The picture I have in my mind is sitting on the dock," Joan Countryman commented, "and there's the sky and there's the trees. And then you have even in a way, a greater sense of space, of being in the wilderness than you do when you're in a grove of trees or something. . . . You could feel a quiet, calm over yourself and others that is very supportive."

As Ann Scattergood Fogg indicated, the power of the community intensified the experience. Meetings also united campers. Writing about her daughter Molly, a Saltash Mountain camper, Mindy Thompson Fullilove, who first came to F&W as a teenage babysitter, commented, "Part of the bond that develops at camp is the connection formed in the intimacy of Meeting." As a result, "strangers" were transformed into "deeply loved friends."[37] Susan Fletcher, an IB camper from a very young age, "loved the community sing and the feeling of togetherness, even though it was overlaid with a lot of Christianity, which it certainly was, and I couldn't sing."[38] Janine Fay said, "It was great being quiet and by the lake. What's not to like, really? It drew us together and got the day going in a good way."

Several campers especially enjoyed the music at meetings. Berl Nussbaum "loved singing hymns." Monteleoni remembered that singing "little hymns from this little blue hymn book which was some kind of Christian hymnbook" constituted an essential part of each day's observance. Kyle Rolnick was nine years old when she first came to IB in 1960. She didn't believe in god, and she didn't like sitting still, but she "loved the hymns." She added that the hymns she learned at camp continued to be important to her as an adult: "I can think of the hymns now and sometimes I actually get a little soothing from some of the hymns that we sang."

Because only 10 percent of the campers were Quakers, we can ask why so many others spoke in such positive terms about the meetings. As we have seen, some focused on specific aspects, which may or may not have had spiritual dimensions. Some campers, however, described powerful spiritual experiences that shaped the rest of their lives. Fullilove herself had been at Farm & Wilderness. "I feel the Great Spirit as a force encircling me, God constantly at my back," she later wrote. "This feeling flows from the daily Meetings that summer I spent at Tamarack Farm."[39] Cathy Wilkerson had attended Quaker meetings before, but for the first time at Indian Brook, they "made sense" to her. She explained how she developed a new understanding of the divine:

> I felt connected as part of the community. I began to think about the way leaders of organized religion used rituals as a device to help people stay together. But maybe, I thought, it was only in the freedom of the trees that people within a community could really feel God's presence. God represented our yearning to be good and to do good things. God was the power of the idea of love that was somehow more than each of our capacities to love. I gave up thinking of God as an entity with a human purpose. It made sense, as the Quakers said, that God was love.[40]

Sally Somers, an IB camper and then a counselor in the late 1950s and early 1960s, wrote, "The combination of being out-of-doors and seeking inspiration in poetry, devotional writings and songs had become my spiritual cornerstone for years."[41]

A few former campers who came from nonreligious backgrounds uncovered spiritual yearnings they could not acknowledge or express at home. Susan Fletcher had been a "red-diaper baby," and because her family was "very grounded in politics and in the here and now," her life had lacked "a spiritual quality." She "had just really, really loved the Quaker meetings, particularly the meetings that we were able to have on the cabin level, where in fact, we planned those meetings and we would pick a theme and bring in poetry, some Psalms, or something that felt a connection to nature." The last, she said, "really, really resonated with me because I hadn't had that in my own life up until then." She never felt drawn to organized religion. When a friend encouraged her to go to a Quaker meeting in Cambridge, where she first lived as a young adult, she had replied, "My problem is that I can never believe in this fantasy that Jesus Christ was the son of God. How could I?" Reassured that Quakers in Cambridge "didn't necessarily believe that," she agreed to attend a meeting. "But it didn't really resonate with me," she said. "So there hasn't been anything organized in my life."

What did remain with Fletcher was her connection with nature. "I would say nature is my God," she continued, "It's my true north, and my favorite poet is Mary Oliver, and I trace all of that back to camp." Five years before she spoke with us, when her daughter underwent breast cancer treatment, Fletcher moved to San Francisco to care for her and her two small children. "And I just found that being able to go out and walk in Golden Gate Park, really helped me in being there for her during that period." She concluded that the spirituality she found at Farm & Wilderness "has been very important to me throughout my life."

Although Rachel Brown Cowan, an IB camper in the 1950s, grew up in a secular family, she converted to Judaism as an adult and then studied at Hebrew Union College. After her ordination as a rabbi, she became well known, especially after founding and directing the Institute for Jewish Spirituality. Before her death in 2018, she told Emily that the first time she realized she could become a spiritual person was when she was at Farm & Wilderness, sitting at a meeting on the dock and observing the nature around her.

Robert Wuthnow's book *After Heaven* helps us understand why other campers may have been open to the meetings' spiritual messages. Wuthnow argues that throughout the 1950s, Americans practiced a "spirituality of dwelling" expressed in institutionalized religion and houses of worship.[42] Church membership grew from 65 million in 1940 to 115 million in 1960, by which time it represented 63 percent of the population.[43] After 1960, a "spirituality of seeking" became increasingly prominent. More and more people abandoned the religion in which they had been raised and stopped attending organized services. Although some became secular, many others sought spiritual insights from various sources.[44] Because a wide variety of Jewish and Christian camps existed, it is perhaps unsurprising that many of the non-Quaker parents who sent their children to F&W had left institutional religion. Joan Countryman's parents "had both been raised in Black Baptist churches" but "were not happy with much of what the church was about." Although her father felt strongly that his children should not be forced into any particular religion, he wanted them to understand what religion was about and had sent them to various Sunday schools. John Wilhelm's mother had resigned from a congregational church because the pastor had refused to relinquish his membership in a segregated country club. "They fought about it for a while, but ultimately he stood his ground," Wilhelm commented. "So I had this kind of bad impression of organized religion. And my limited experience of Quakerism at Tamarack Farm was like a breath of fresh air." He added, "I really loved morning meeting." After the interview, he sent us a copy of a photograph that still hung on his bedroom wall of a morning meeting he had attended at Tamarack Farm.

Our own experience can serve as another example. We are certain that our parents never would have considered sending us to any of the Jewish camps that had emerged in the 1940s and 1950s. Judaism was what our father had most wanted to flee when he left his immigrant parents' home to seek higher education. Our mother, however, was different. Despite our father's contempt for religion, she always found ways to convey to her daughters (though not her sons) how important it was to her. She took us to High Holiday (Rosh Hashanah and Yom Kippur) services at the local temple and insisted that we attend classes there. Raging against the rabbi for his lack of insights, she let us know that religious figures

FIGURE 10. A "silent meeting" at Tamarack Farm. Photo courtesy of John Wilhelm.

should dispense wisdom and offer succor for life's difficulties. But it was the Zionism the temple espoused that finally forced her to sever her ties with it and stop attending any Jewish services. Although none of her daughters looked for an alternative religion or embarked on anything resembling a religious quest, we had had enough experience to be able to appreciate a silent Quaker meeting.

Liz Ohle, who came to Indian Brook as a counselor in the 1970s, had already turned away from an organized religion.[45] Among those with whom we spoke, she was one of the very few members of the F&W community who found a new home in Quakerism. In a 2019 sermon, Ohle chronicled her spiritual odyssey. "My parents were devoted church-goers and participated fully in the life of their church," she recalled. "They were very moral and ethical people and believed that being of service was a high calling. . . . But their specific religious beliefs weren't part of our family life, except as demonstrated in a few rituals including saying grace before dinner and saying bedtime prayers with my dad when I was young." She joined the youth group primarily to remain in touch with her friends. At one point, however, the group asked a critical question: "How could church members call themselves Christian if there was unaddressed poverty or racism or inequality in our city and neighborhoods?" Two speakers who visited the church provided Ohle with an example of the kind of religious experience she wanted: "What impressed me about both of these speakers was that their religion permeated their lives, not just when they were in their church building. They lived with conviction, trying to be true to their religious beliefs." When she left home at seventeen to go to college, she became involved in social movements of the 1960s. One Sunday, she attended a church service but found it "sorely lacking" and never returned.

But then in 1977, "at the age of 24," she continued,

> I began working at a New England summer camp called Farm and Wilderness. My sister was working there and invited me to join her. Somewhere in the application process, I learned it was a Quaker camp, but had no idea what that meant. My sister was pretty cool so I figured that a Quaker camp must be cool. And it was! This began my official Quaker journey. . . . Though surrounded by fidgeting and squirming 9 to 14 year olds, the gathering in the circle was peaceful and powerful. I loved having the daily experience at camp acquaint me with a spiritual practice I have carried with me ever since.[46]

Ohle worked at Indian Brook for fifteen years, as a counselor and director. After the first few summers, she began to look for a Quaker meeting to join and has considered herself a Quaker ever since.

Some F&W alumni who felt drawn to Quakerism developed more eclectic religious beliefs. Peg Espinola, an IB camper in the late 1940s, for example, described herself on her college application as "Jewish with Quaker leanings."[47] She now self-identifies as a "'Juudhist Bu'—a Jewish Unitarian with Buddhist leanings." Others expressed their admiration for Quakerism by choosing to attend a Quaker college, typically Earlham or Swarthmore, working for the American Friends Service Committee, or occasionally attending a Quaker meeting. "Over the years from time to time, I stepped in at a Quaker meeting," Judy Polumbaum said, "but I never joined a Quaker meeting house or anything like that. I guess I'm not disciplined enough. But I think it is a wonderful concept."

Yet other former campers and staff said that F&W's morning meetings helped them develop spiritual practices based, at least partly, on meditation. Anne McElhinney, whose background was Presbyterian, began to work at Tamarack Farm in the 1970s. "Being introduced to this concept of sitting in silence," she commented, "it really struck a note with me. It was incredible. It kind of changed the direction of my life or it gave direction to my life."[48] After leaving the camps, she joined first a meditation group and then a commune, where she spent seven years meditating every day, morning and evening. She now identifies as Buddhist. Janine Fay said that the meetings made her "open" to sitting in silence; they were "like meditation," which had become an important ingredient of her spiritual life. Kyle Rolnick, who still found the hymns she learned at IB soothing, told us that although she does not consider herself to be "spiritual," she meditates daily.

FRIENDSHIP

Summer camps provide the setting for numerous young adult novels. Several themes predominate. Separated from family and friends for the first time, the campers take risks, reassess their own capabilities, and gradually grow physically and emotionally stronger. The creation of friendships constitutes an essential part of this process of transformation. Occasionally it is at camp that a young girl or boy forms friendships for the first time.[49] Occasionally, a new friend is someone the camper initially disliked or mistrusted.[50] Occasionally, new friends have characteristics that would make them unlikely companions at home.[51] As campers recognize their own capacities, they learn to trust and admire people they might otherwise have ignored. They also discover that others appreciate them.

Although those we interviewed did not describe their experiences with all the drama conveyed in young adult literature, they frequently commented on the friendships that began in summers at F&W. Many, like Jon Jacques, told us that those friendships persisted into adulthood. Jane Wohl, for example, recalled not only that Emily had been her counselor one year but also that she had remained close friends with a camper she met the same summer.[52] Neil Rolnick cherishes his relationships with "a bunch of friends who are really close, who have been with me all these years." He continued, "So that's really remarkable, to have that kind of connection and to share that. . . . And really, virtually all of the serious romantic relationships that I've had in my life, have been with people I met at camp. So that's all really positive." Helen Seitz, who had been at Indian Brook in 1950, commented, "Every friend I had from that time on either was [someone I met at] camp or [someone I met through] somebody I knew at camp."[53] Jean Coulter Brown wrote to us that after camp she shared a house with two former campers—Janine Fay and Jane Ehrlich Bayer—and "stayed in touch with other campers as well." Those friendships, she added, "felt like an extended family and filled any gap of loneliness."[54] And Nate Hausman, who attended F&W a generation after Brown, said, "My very best friends in the world are still, you know, folks I met . . . as campers at Flying Cloud."[55]

We, too, count friendships among the most meaningful legacies of our time at F&W. Emily met Connie Brown at Tamarack Farm in 1957. Three years later, they were roommates at Swarthmore. Although they now live on different coasts, they manage to see each other a few times a year. The picture of Peggy and Jane Ehrlich Bayer, taken in 1956, shows the folds from having been in Peggy's wallet for many years. In the mid-1970s, Jane was diagnosed with breast cancer. During the years she was sick, Peggy was one among many former campers who helped care for her, her husband, Carl, and their two children, Zach and Emily. At least half a dozen men and women who had been at camp together came to her funeral in 1985 (as did Susan Webb, who had known Jane since she was a little girl). After the pandemic began, Peggy joined many of these people on Zoom once a month. She also has gathered with campers who attended Tamarack Farm in 1960 for a fiftieth reunion at the home of Janine Fay in 2010 and a virtual sixtieth one a decade later.

CONCLUSION

Ken Webb frequently asserted that camps could transform children by inculcating certain values. Listening to former campers, however, we learned that many families attracted to the Farm & Wilderness camps already subscribed to those values. Children who felt isolated in the conformist culture surrounding them in the post–World War II era found a sense of community at F&W. There they created the personal bonds and strengthened the convictions that enabled them to join activist groups seeking fundamental social change in the 1960s and early 1970s.

Because large numbers of religious camps existed, parents who wanted to deepen their children's understanding of a specific faith tradition were unlikely to choose F&W. Some alumni we spoke to had little interest in the morning meetings for worship and attended them only under duress. Many others,

FIGURE 11. Peggy Klein and Jane Ehrlich at the fair in 1956. Photograph courtesy of Margaret Nelson.

however, remember the meetings as a central element of camp life. Alienated by institutional religions, they found meaning in spiritual experiences in nature.

We claim nothing unique about F&W when we talk about friendships, even if the intimacies forged when we sang together, sat at meetings, and argued about politics felt special at the time.

4 · GENDER AND SEXUAL ORIENTATION

Like American society in general, Farm & Wilderness in the 1940s, 1950s, and early 1960s emphasized gender distinctions. Neither Timberlake nor Indian Brook, however, conformed precisely to prevailing norms. Timberlake stressed physical strength and competence but not the competition that characterized many other boys' organizations. Indian Brook embraced a more expansive view of women's capabilities than was current at the time. That camp changed the most in the period we examine. With the emergence of the women's movement, it became explicitly feminist. In addition, it took a leading role in grappling with the issue of sexual orientation in the late 1970s.

WOMEN AT WORK AT INDIAN BROOK

When Susan and Ken Webb wrote the first Indian Brook brochure in 1941, they promised the parents of the twenty girls they hoped to attract that the program would give them "self reliance, sturdy health, responsibility and training in useful skills." The campers would be involved in "gay sports and play," and could "help with cooking and candy making, simple canning" (along with "plenty of outdoor camp cooking also"). In addition, they would "learn how to 'keep house' in one of the cottages, sweeping, dusting and making beds." Other activities would include "gardens, poultry to take care of . . . knitting for the Red Cross, making dolls' clothes, haying . . . swimming and water sports, hiking, [and] trip camping."[1] Clearly, in those early years, Susan (if not Susan and Ken) wanted to reassure parents that the girls would be able to acquire the skills necessary to run a home as a wife and mother as well as engage in some of the more vigorous, outdoor activities already offered to their brothers at Timberlake.

Those reassurances adhered to the reigning culture. Historian Leslie Paris writes that the "earliest camp directors assumed that the gendered segregation of campers was natural and appropriate." Boys' camps, she adds, would be "masculine retreats from an overly feminized world," while girls' camps would offer "parallel camping experiences."[2] But parallel did not mean the same. If on the one hand, the Camp Fire Girls program, which provided the basis for many girls' camps at the start of the twentieth century, offered participation in outdoor life, it also "explicitly tied participation in outdoor life to older ideologies of maternal devotion and domestic inclination."[3] Women should gain strength because they would then have greater "childbearing and nurturing capabilities." In addition, camping would "buttress traditional female skills." The Native American cultural elements that were included in camping were designed to further grace domesticity, not expose girls to "savagery." Similarly, the Girl Scouts offered badges for "domestic labor, like nursing and laundry."[4]

By the mid-1950s, when we first arrived at Indian Brook (IB), the camp was a very different place from the one the Webbs had initially envisioned. In 1955, an article in the *Lightning Bug* captures the decreased emphasis on domesticity. The author had observed Indian Brook girls who had been involved in a project to be sent overseas to children in "India, Korea, Europe and wherever parcels are being sent." After listing the separate activities of each cabin, the author suggested that the girls could handle physical activities with aplomb but had more difficulty with "domestic arts": "It's been amusing to see the girls after they've come back from 20 mile hikes and swam to Bear Pit and back (1½ miles) sitting quietly in their cabins knitting lumpy squares and sewing uneven lines but looking thoroughly domesticated."[5] In 2019, an interviewer asked Joan Cannady Countryman, an Indian Brook camper in the early 1950s, about her years directing the Lincoln School, an all-girls school in Providence, Rhode Island. She responded that she wanted to convince girls that they could do anything, explaining that she "had had that experience at Sarah Lawrence [her undergraduate college] and also at Farm & Wilderness. You know I went to the girls' camp where we built privies and things. I was ready to fight with anybody who said girls can't do things."[6]

One of the unusual things Indian Brook girls could do in the 1950s and early 1960s was wield an axe. Jane Wohl told us that when she returned home after her first summer at Indian Brook in 1960, the family's coal furnace went out.[7] Following her mother down to the basement, Wohl watched as she tried unsuccessfully to light the fire with two-by-fours. Taking an axe, Wohl showed her mother how to split the wood for kindling. "She was very impressed," Wohl recalled. Martyne Stout, who first went to IB in 1961, encountered a different response. "When my mother learned that I had used an axe in my first summer," Stout said, "she didn't want me to return. She said, 'She's not going back there.' I wanted to help my dad split wood for the fireplace. My mom put up a big fuss, but in the end, my dad won, and I came back."[8]

It may be impossible to recognize how remarkable Indian Brook was without understanding what was available to White, middle-class girls in the post–World War II era. They could be cheerleaders, but in the age before Title IX, most organized sports were closed to them. They could flirt but must contain male sexuality. "The boy is expected to ask for as much as possible, the girl to yield as little as possible," wrote the anthropologist Margaret Mead.[9] Abortion was illegal; girls who found themselves pregnant were shuffled off to places like the Florence Crittenden Homes where they were essentially forced to relinquish their babies.[10]

If teenage girls looked to the future, they would find no support for a broader vision of what they might become. Fired from the workforce after World War II, women encountered many forms of discrimination. Banks denied them loans, most bars refused to serve them, and some states excluded them from jury duty. Women represented a tiny fraction of all lawyers or doctors. Few people believed the testimony of rape survivors, assuming that they "had asked for it." Women's marital status determined whether they were called "Miss" or "Mrs." and even, within the middle class, whether or not they worked outside the home. In our family, our mother's regular production of published mysteries was considered her "hobby," occasionally celebrated in the local newspaper by a picture showing her among her five children. As the older ones began to leave home for college (and marriage), our mother obtained an MA from Teachers College in NYC and found a job teaching English in a nearby high school. Our father made that work impossible: he declared that she embarrassed him by suggesting that he couldn't support his family, and he certainly picked up none of the housework to ease her burden. Although she loved the work, she lasted only a year or two.

A 2013 *Washington Post* article titled "Answering Harvard's Question about My Personal Life, 52 Years Later" by Phyllis Richman reminds us how unusual our mother was in getting an advanced degree. When Richman applied to the Harvard School of Urban Planning in 1961, she received a letter asking how she would balance a career with her "responsibilities" to her husband and future children. Addressing the professor who had written to her, Richman first apologized for not responding sooner but explained she had been very busy. "Your letter left me down but not out," she continued. "Before your letter, it hadn't occurred to me that marriage could hinder my acceptance at Harvard or my career. I was so discouraged by it that I don't think I ever completed the application, yet I was too intimidated to contradict you when we met face to face."[11]

Like many women who encounter obstacles in one field, Richman eventually built a successful career in another. She wrote that "having children in my late 20s, while I was developing my career, and bartering for babysitting, carpooling, and cooking made my life complicated—but also encouraged me to be resilient and flexible." In 1976, she became the *Washington Post* restaurant critic, a position she held for twenty-three years. She also is the author of several books.[12] Richman's 2013 article attracted responses from many women who recalled they had had similar experiences half a century earlier. Two had encountered barriers at the undergraduate level. A mere decade before 1975, when Peggy began teaching at Middlebury College as one of the very few women on the faculty, one applicant there had been told that although she was a strong candidate for admission, she should not apply for the scholarship she needed because the college preferred to invest in men. The other had been a junior at Purdue when administrators discovered she was married and withdrew her scholarship. When she complained, they informed her that she could drop out and support her husband, another Purdue student.[13]

A 1977 book titled *Working It Out: 23 Women Writers, Artists, Scientists, and Scholars Talk about Their Lives and Work*, edited by Sara Ruddick and Pamela Daniels, provides further evidence that Richman's experience was commonplace.[14] Many writers described the discrimination they encountered in higher education. For example, after a brilliant undergraduate career at Brandeis, Evelyn Fox Keller entered Harvard's physics department in 1957 expecting she would continue to shine. Instead, she began "two years of almost unmitigated provocation, insult, and denial."[15] Both professors and fellow students assumed she could not understand difficult concepts. When she turned in an excellent paper, the professor accused her of plagiarism. Although she loved physics, she decided to switch to molecular biology in the middle of her second year.[16]

The strictures on female lives may help explain why so many women we interviewed who had been at Indian Brook in the 1950s and early 1960s emphasized the sense of freedom they had experienced there. "In the morning," Ann Scattergood Fogg, an IB camper in the early 1950s, recalled, "you had work projects or you had swimming or you had some specific thing that you went to, but the afternoons were kind of wide open and you could really do anything. I mean, there were lots of activities offered, but you could do just about anything you wanted. It was wonderful, it was so different from school. I just felt so totally comfortable. It wasn't that I had a terrible time in school, but there was something about the openness of [camp] that was just incredible."[17] Carol Rapaport Monteleoni was homesick the first year she went to IB as a young girl but, she added, "I liked the activities, and I liked the kids, and I loved running around barefoot and just all the stuff we did."[18] In 1958, at IB, being barefoot made Janine Fay feel like "I'm open, I'm open to taking stuff in."[19] Martyne Stout told us that although she never heard the word "tomboy" as a child, she fit the profile.[20] "But my mother," she continued "was sort of a Southern Belle type and was just in despair because all I did was hang off of trees, upside down, ride my bike, and get dirty." Martyne wanted to "be in the outdoors, not having to worry about going to a very strict Bible school, wearing gloves. . . . And at camp [IB in 1961] I had found my place." We, too, remember the joy of jettisoning constricting clothes. Going to junior and senior high school, we donned straight skirts, stockings, girdles, and pointed brassieres. Even at Swarthmore College in the early 1960s, a dress code required us to wear skirts to dinner every night except Sunday. But at camp, we wore shorts or jeans, lumber jackets and sweat shirts. Mirrors made an appearance only when we were getting ready for square dances. (But even there, we continued to go barefoot and wear loose clothes; straight skirts and heels would not work on the dance floor at the TL lodge or on the grounds at the annual fair.)

From the start, Susan had been aware of the importance of having a separate place for girls to acquire skills. She had noticed that "when girls were in activities with boys they soon found themselves doing the chores and the dishes; they simply didn't get a chance to learn skills for themselves. As one simple example: when girls began to chop wood the boys would soon take over. We felt that girls needed to realize that they could be just as expert in the same skills as boys and could learn to be competent individuals on their own. Independent women was a goal." If not her only original concern, Susan hoped that Indian Brook would

FIGURE 12. Square dancing at the fair. Photograph courtesy of Berl Nusbaum and photographed by Jack Nussbaum.

"give girls the feeling that they could be as rugged as the boys and do anything Timberlake offered."[21]

But if Indian Brook had long offered girls more opportunities than they could find elsewhere, the women's movement still had a powerful impact. Susan's hopes for girls infused camp policy, but she never stated them explicitly. Although Jane Wohl showed her mother how to use an axe, most of us assumed that the skills we acquired at camp did not follow us home. If we learned to use our bodies in new ways at camp, we experienced that as something special but temporary, with no counterpart in our "real" lives. Subsequent generations of campers could integrate their camp experiences with developments in society as a whole. Posting "Women at Work" signs, they increasingly viewed themselves as feminists. In addition, girls began to engage in activities previously associated with boys alone. Although Ken Webb had preached the virtues of the "Fifth Freedom" for everyone, it had been restricted to "skinny-dipping" during free swim at Indian Brook; now girls argued that they, too, should be able to shed clothes whenever they were at the waterfront. For the first time, girls also built and lit the bonfire that marked the end of the annual fair.

The departure of John Stevens, the head of work projects at Indian Brook, enabled the campers to develop a new set of skills without male supervision. Liz Ohle arrived in 1977 after John Stevens no longer worked for F&W.[22] Although she did not ask to fill the vacuum he had left, she soon discovered that she could use the absence of male staff to promote girls' empowerment. She herself had a lot to learn. She recalled that when her sister, Janet Green, who was the IB director at the time, asked her to join the work projects staff, "we knew nothing. We were handed like a 15-page tool inventory. We didn't know what nine-tenth of those tools were. We had to go through the tool room and get an instruction book from the library about tools and had to learn the difference between a slotted screw and a Philips head screw and three different kinds of hammers and just all the things." Having decided that the staff should build a composting KYBO, Green found a blueprint and asked Ohle to take charge. "So over the next four weeks," Ohle "learned how to prepare a foundation, how to pour concrete, how to lay cinderblock, how to mix mortar, how to read a blueprint for a relatively simple structure." Although she had never done any of those things before, she was not deterred: "I knew how to sew, I knew how to cook, I knew how to follow a pattern." And she realized that construction did not require "inaccessible information" but rather that the knowledge had been kept "a mystery for women."

At the end of the summer, Ohle was appointed head of work projects. When she returned the following year, Green asked her not only to finish the KYBO but also to start a cabin. Ohle told us that she said at the time, "No man is going to drive one nail into this cabin because we will give away our accomplishments if we do that. You may think about times in your life when it seems like you did something and then somebody else got the credit. Maybe you didn't even think about it. But I am going to tell you, we are going to own this cabin." Ohle added that building the cabin "was amazing, really amazing" because "it required some skills women were not expected to have." Although "there was this sense of purity about using hand tools for everything" at F&W, she was "adamant that girls needed to learn how to handle noisy, powerful tools." She ran extension cords from the main lodge so they could use "a skill saw to cut the floorboards, cut the rafters, cut the joists, cut the wall studs. Girls needed to learn how to do that, if the girls were going to be empowered and carry that empowerment home with them." The second to last day of camp, she said, "we nailed down the last floorboard. We had dug eight foundation holes in that rocky, Vermont soil. You had to dig below frostline, so we did that. . . . We learned how to make everything level and square and straight . . . we did all that. And then we got the joists and we put those on and joist hangers. What the hell is a joist hanger? We learned about joist hangers. We learned, you know, just every single step was a massive learning curve."

After the campers left, Ohle and her staff stayed for several weeks to continue the work. She described their achievements: "We got all the walls done, we got the sliding up, we got the roof rafters done, we got the bunks built, we got all that stuff done." The following spring, a few weeks before the camp reopened, Ohle and her staff finished the rest of the work "so kids moved in there that year. They were so proud." The one remaining job was to name the cabin. Rejecting all the "cute" names from "Winnie the Pooh" that were common at Indian Brook, they chose "Sojourner Truth," a label "that gave that cabin some power."

TIMBERLAKE'S VERSION OF MASCULINITY

Although Indian Brook sought to help girls acquire the skills and traits commonly associated with men, Timberlake did not reciprocate. As we have seen, Ken wanted to make his boys tougher, more muscular, and more self-confident, not sensitive, empathetic, or caring. Like Susan, he believed sex segregation was essential but for a very different reason. He wrote in *Summer Magic* that separate camps allowed boys to "have their sports without the girls 'getting in their hair,'" while permitting girls to "be as unrestrainedly feminine as they want."[23] Indeed, at a time when Indian Brook was enabling girls to resist prevailing gender norms, Ken suggested that they needed to practice the feminine arts. A girl he called "Sally" did "about everything one should not do if she wants to win friends and influence people." She was not only "ungracious in manner, rebellious, and selfish," but also "unkempt" and "sloppy in dress." After Sally poured out her heart about a divorce in the family to a caring counselor, the counselor recommended that she clean herself up, comb her hair, and put on a "nice dress to remind yourself of what you want to be. Then keep yourself tidied up." Over time, with the help of the staff, "Sally began to have more respect for herself as her greater care in grooming would indicate." The story's conclusion continued to focus on her appearance: "Sally never would be a pretty girl, but there was a certain vivacity, a charming intentness at times in her manner which enhanced the natural attractiveness of youth and good health."[24]

Ken also exhibited the culture's contempt for mothers. Leslie Paris writes that camp directors in the first half of the twentieth century were concerned about "so called sissies, those boys who appear weak or effeminate, most at risk of becoming homosexuals, and most in need of outdoor activity." Like many others at the time, camp leaders blamed mothers "for their sons' supposed lack of masculinity." Mother blaming reached its height in the 1940s and 1950s. Philip Wylie's *Generation of Vipers*, which argued that "Mom" had "enfeebled a nation of once free and dreaming men," sold fifty thousand copies between 1943 and 1955.[25] That year, the book was in its twentieth printing, and the American Library Association designated it one of the major nonfiction works of the first half of the twentieth century.[26] In *Summer Magic*, published in 1953, Ken wrote about a boy who refused to go on a hike: "Even the sobriquet of 'cream puff' bestowed on him by his cabin mates . . . had no effect, or rather it drove him to refuge where he had always found it: he telephoned his mother. Mother told him, so he informed his counselor, that he didn't have to go on a hike if he didn't want to!"[27] The book also pointed to the many mothers who were reluctant to send their sons away, fearing that they were too young, but who were delighted when they received back "a youngster whose glance is more self reliant, whose shoulders are straighter, whose whole bearing betokens a new-found confidence."[28] In general, Ken indicated that one of the major virtues of camp was the "de-mothering" that occurred.[29]

But Ken departed from prevailing norms by seeking to create an environment for boys that was free from the usual sources of competition. Timberlake offered no tennis lessons, baseball games, or color wars. Instead, campers had opportunities to develop individual skills, in areas like campcraft, and to gain a sense of physical competence, through activities like hiking and canoeing. Some boys found the absence of competition a great relief from the pressures they endured at home. One staff member, however, considered it ridiculous. Martyne Stout, who occupied various roles at F&W for many years, told us that her husband worked at Timberlake for two summers as the head of the waterfront. He quit because he was a competitive swimmer and said, "I just don't get it. . . . They play games, and they don't care who wins? What's the point?" Of course, competition inevitably crept in. One former camper told us that because boys received awards for campcraft at the banquet marking the end of camp, those who reached the highest level considered themselves part of an "exclusive society." He added that some boys would even "cheat" to achieve a desired level. As we will see in chapter 8, the Indian lore program selected some boys but not others to join a special "tribe."

As F&W expanded, it offered boys a greater range of opportunities and, often, better resources than the girls. Saltash Mountain Camp (SAM), originally for boys alone, had access to Lake Ninevah; Dark Meadow, for girls, had no waterfront at all. Flying Cloud (FC), the second of the outpost camps, and in many ways the fulfillment of Ken's idealization of ruggedness, served only boys. Girls noticed this disparity. "Sometimes I wish that there were an FC for girls," Mindy Thompson Fullilove's daughter Molly wrote in a letter home from SAM. Molly hoped to direct such a camp should it ever materialize.[30] Sarah Yahn, who became an independent producer as an adult, had also been jealous. "I went to Indian Brook and Tamarack Farm, but I really wanted to go to Flying Cloud, the boys-only Indian camp," where the campers engaged in "what looked to me like the best and most important 'let's pretend' ever."[31]

SEXUALITY

After the Farm & Wilderness community learned about the child molestation that had occurred at Timberlake for many years, some former campers began to wonder to what extent Ken had been aware of it and even if he had been implicated in some way. In public, however, he expressed views that were prevalent in the 1950s and 1960s, insisting that sex of any sort should occur only between married heterosexuals. Historian Elaine Tyler May notes that postwar experts "believed that premarital sexual experimentation was taking place to such an extent that calls for abstinence would be futile. The goal now was to teach young people already indulging in 'petting' how to keep sex under control."[32] Fearful that "petting" would lead to promiscuity after marriage and, ultimately to divorce, Ken instructed campers to avoid it altogether and to focus on waiting "for the proper time."[33] Although Ken accepted coeducation among older children (at Tamarack Farm) in 1973, he continued to discourage sexual activity. He encouraged the boys and girls at Tamarack Farm to swim without wearing bathing suits but insisted that nudity at the waterfront would create healthy interaction without being unduly sexually stimulating.[34] He was silent about homosexuality and, of course, the possibility of sexual abuse.

Susan made it clear that sexuality of any kind was unacceptable at Indian Brook. Peg Espinola, who had been there in the late 1940s, remembered Susan "bawling out a camper who had sat on her boyfriend's lap. She said that was absolutely not okay."[35] This episode stood out for Peg in part because Susan's tone of voice contrasted so greatly with her normal demeanor: "Susan Webb generally spoke in a calm voice, but on that occasion she was quite dramatic and expressed disbelief that the two campers did not understand what could be wrong with their behavior!" Indian Brook campers from the 1950s remember that when, after coed events, they walked with their boyfriends along the dirt road leading back to their cabins, Susan would come along in her station wagon and urge the girls to ride the rest of the way. One woman laughingly told us, "Couples soon learned to dive into the bushes when they heard a car approaching."[36]

According to the interviews we conducted, Susan and her counselors also seemed to have had their antennae out about the possibility of the molestation of girls by older women. A former camper recounted her experience of being "cuddled" in her bed by a member of the staff, at age ten or eleven, after she had reported being homesick.[37] Apparently, someone observed this event; the next day, the staff member was gone. But neither Susan nor any members of her staff openly discussed lesbian relationships. As campers, we were encouraged to "pretty" ourselves for the coed square dances; the rest of the time, we were treated as asexual beings. Within two decades, that would change.

SEXUAL ORIENTATION

In the late 1970s, the Indian Brook leadership launched a campaign to increase the visibility of the issue of sexual orientation. Once again, Liz Ohle, IB director between 1986 and 1991, is central to the story. "People think that openness happens overnight, that it happens quickly," she said to us.[38] "Or people assume that, 'Well, sure, F&W has always been like that.' And it's just not true. There were other places in the world where one would go if somebody wanted to live with an openness about their identity as a lesbian." Ohle discovered how unusual and courageous her campaign had been when she published an article titled "Putting Everyone in the Picture: Countering Homophobia in the Camp Setting" in the November/December 1990 issue of Camping Magazine, the official organ of the American Camp Association (ACA).[39] The entire issue focused on diversity: "The one area of diversity often avoided by camps is that of sexual orientation," Ohle wrote. "It is difficult to celebrate an invisible difference. Because of social stereotypes, many have been afraid to openly acknowledge and accept gay males and lesbians either as campers or as staff. We hope that the gay people around us will keep it to themselves. But by addressing our fears and learning the truths rather than the myths about gay people, our camp communities can be enriched further, since no one would have to hide or pretend not to see."

Although the ACA journal rarely received letters to the editor, comments about Ohle's article poured in. The eight letters that appeared in the February issue were deeply hostile. One camp director, for example, wrote, "Perhaps it would have been wiser for Ms. Ohle to direct her suggestions more restrictedly toward those camps who do not try to mirror the standards of the Scriptures."

Another wrote, "I do not believe that camp is the place to 'educate' children and staff about sexual orientation. Period." Yet another stated that he would not renew his 1991 membership in ACA unless he received "absolute assurance that ACA does not support or condone the staff of homosexuals in member youth camps."[40] Ohle had to wait until the March issue to read a few positive comments (along with more negative ones). The whole experience, she told us, had been "brutal."

By 1990, homosexuality had been one of the most fiercely contested issues in American culture and politics for a little more than two decades. Most historians agree that the conflict between protestors and police following the June 1969 raid of the Stonewall Inn in Greenwich Village marked the beginning of the gay liberation movement. A few months earlier, Carl Wittman had drafted "A Gay Manifesto," which historian Michael Bronski calls the "defining document" of the movement:

1. Free ourselves: come out everywhere; initiate self defense and political activity, initiate counter community institutions.
2. Turn other gay people on: talk all the time; understand, forgive, accept.
3. Free the homosexual in everyone: we'll be getting a good bit of shit from threatened latents: be gentle, and keep talking & act free.
4. We've been playing an act for a long time, so we're consummate actors. Now we can begin to be, and it'll be a good show![41]

Throughout the 1970s, the movement achieved significant victories. In 1973, the American Psychiatric Association voted to drop homosexuality from the *Diagnostic and Statistical Manual of Mental Disorders* (DSM). By 1976, twenty-nine U.S. cities had passed nondiscrimination laws that added sexual orientation to the Civil Rights Act of 1964.[42] But the movement also engendered a significant backlash, much of which focused on children. In 1977, Anita Bryant, an entertainer and Miss America runner-up, founded a Christian group called Save Our Children to overturn the nondiscrimination act in Miami, Florida. The following year, California state senator John Briggs proposed "Proposition 6" to prohibit lesbians and gay men, as well as any teacher who was discovered "advocating, imposing, encouraging, or promoting" homosexuality, from teaching in public schools. Although the months-long campaign by lesbian and gay activists to defeat the proposition eventually succeeded, the widespread support it initially garnered helps explain why the issue of gay and lesbian counselors at summer camps raised such powerful emotions.

Aware of the broader social context, Ohle initially took what she called "discreet" steps to increase the visibility of lesbians at Indian Brook. She understood that Farm & Wilderness was "not in a financial position to take a highly controversial position. When you have an issue that is likely to have a potentially damaging impact on the camps you move thoughtfully and slowly, but never losing the perspective of where you want to be heading. And so I think that's what we did." She first discussed sexual orientation at a staff training before campers arrived in the mid- or late 1970s. "We knew that some of the issues that came up in women's communities outside of camp were apt to percolate below the surface. So we addressed some of the concerns or issues around lesbianism. There wasn't a huge amount of societal information that would have accurately reflected what it meant to be a lesbian in a deeper sense."

Some of the concerns Ohle mentioned also inflamed women's organizations, leading to what was often called the "gay-straight" split. As historians John D'Emilio and Estelle B. Freedman write, "Many feminists sensitive to the reaction that the [gay] movement was eliciting in the minds of Americans sought to keep the issue [of lesbianism] quiet, to push lesbians out of sight."[43] Betty Friedan, the founder of the National Organization for Women (NOW), was particularly anxious about what she referred to as "the Lavender Menace," fearful that lesbians would give feminism a bad name.[44] Ohle, however, received support from the Indian Brook community. Ann Scattergood Fogg, an IB staff member at the time, remembered the discussions Ohle led "as an eye opener for me. I hadn't really done much thinking about women as lesbians. I mean it was perfectly fine with me, but I hadn't known about people being discriminated against. I heard them talking, and that was new to me."[45]

With the emergence of the HIV/AIDS epidemic in the early 1980s, all gays and lesbians came under attack. Because the first victims were gay men, the right used the disease to condemn all homosexuals. The headline on the cover of an issue of Jerry Falwell's *Moral Majority Report* read, "Homosexual Diseases Threaten American Families."[46] Even liberal magazines referred to HIV/AIDS as the "gay plague."[47] Ohle responded in various ways. She invited an AIDS educator in Vermont to speak to IB girls. When panels of the AIDS quilt, created to memorialize all those who died of AIDS, circulated through the country, Ohle asked that one come to the camp and then hung it in the main lodge. "It had a 'powerful' impact," she told us because "we're talking about the years of the AIDS pariah and the absolute loss of an entire generation of gay men and fears about it and lack of knowledge."

In addition, she organized a support group for girls who had gay and lesbian parents. "We knew they couldn't even feel safe to tell their cabin mates," she commented to us. "I mean, homophobia was huge. It was big. And they knew how to be in the closet. They knew they weren't going to become friends, but they knew each other existed and they knew they weren't alone, and they knew there were people in the community that got it." Soon afterward, she invited a former IB camper with two mothers to speak to the older girls. Ohle remembered being "scared to death," knowing that "not every parent of every camper was going to be thrilled about this." But "it worked out well."

When we asked Ohle how she thought the growing visibility of lesbians at Indian Brook had affected enrollment, she acknowledged that some parents undoubtedly became reluctant to send their girls. We will see in chapter 6 that Ken Webb insisted that his efforts to integrate F&W enabled him to attract just the clientele he wanted. Similarly, Ohle added that IB parents during her leadership were a self-selected group who supported her endeavor.

Anne McElhinney, a Tamarack Farm counselor beginning in the early 1970s, said that unlike Indian Brook, Timberlake "seemed oblivious" to the issue of sexual orientation for many years. Tamarack Farm was a different story.[48] When McElhinney first worked there, she did not acknowledge her sexuality, even to herself. Like many other lesbians, she came out later in that decade. Returning to the Farm in 1980, she had to decide when and how to come out to others. She did so first with a couple of campers while she was working with them on the roof of the farmhouse because "it just seemed easy and seemed appropriate." A showing of the film about Harvey Milk provided another opportunity. (The first openly gay man to be elected to public office in California, Milk was assassinated in 1978.) When the film ended, McElhinney disclosed her identity to the entire camp, because, she said, "how could you not" when the film's message was "come out, come out, wherever you are." The campers were nonplussed: "Of course it was no big deal for anybody. They all just applauded, and it was sweet and then that was that." One colleague remembered that McElhinney had "changed my world" with regard to lesbian issues.

Len Cadwallader, who became executive director in 1985, also linked Ken and Susan's racial integration efforts with innovations surrounding sexual orientation: "So there definitely are things like race relations that the Webb's embraced, that we in turn embraced when it became an issue of sexual orientation. And we said, 'We're proud to be a part of what's happening in our country.' And we want the campers, the young people who are coming to Farm & Wilderness to be at a place where it can be comfortable just talking about these thing and acknowledging them. . . . Ken and Susan talked about camping from the neck up. So we weren't afraid of dealing with social issues."[49] Another camp director also drew a connection between the longtime leadership of the camps on issues of racial justice and its pioneering actions on the topic of gender. "You know, it's not a competition," he said, "[but] I felt like we're ahead of the head of the curve on a number of issues, first racially, and then on a gender issue. And that was part of the beauty of the place. I mean, the biggest part of the beauty of the place."[50]

The changing attitudes around gender and sexuality did not please everyone. A few former campers we interviewed suggested that the feminism at IB in the late 1970s and early 1980s became didactic and formulaic rather than a simple guide that campers could easily integrate into their daily lives. One mother, who had attended IB in the 1950s, recalled that her daughter begged to be allowed to come home when she was challenged to explore her attitudes toward her own body. When an older cousin traveled to F&W to pick her up, the "no males" policy forced him to leave.

CONCLUSION

Although IB had always sought to empower girls, it changed dramatically in the 1970s and 1980s as "Women at Work" signs appeared, making the camp a place of dynamic feminism rather than one that offered implicit respect for women's capabilities. One woman, who joined the IB staff during those years, remembered that "there was definitely a feeling of 'We are powerful and darn it, you're going to be powerful.'"[51] Changing attitudes also shaped the experience of campers at Tamarack Farm. Anne McElhinney recalled, as an example, that the girls confronted the boys about their choice of music marked by the language of sex and violence and convinced them to practice some other songs. Our interviews suggest these shifts had little or no impact on Timberlake. The following chapter may help explain why.

5 · SEXUAL ABUSE

Much of what we have written so far resonates with our own experiences and that of our friends. From our own children, nieces and nephews, and the children of friends, we learned about the ways in which the camps sought to remain true to their original vision while changing, particularly around issues of gender and sexual orientation (as we have just seen) and race and ethnicity (as we discuss in the next two chapters).

But it was not until the mid-1990s that we learned about sexual abuse at Timberlake, although our brothers, born four and six years after Peggy, had had intimations that something was not right there.[1] Our younger brother, in particular, had been wary enough about the counselor assigned to his cabin that, along with a friend, he sought guidance from another counselor he knew. That man told the boys that they should come to him should anything untoward happen; they were greatly relieved when their counselor was suddenly removed from the cabin and assigned only to waterfront duty. In retrospect, this seems like a particularly odd assignment, since there he would have access to boys swimming without bathing suits. What is perhaps even more astonishing is that this issue was never discussed in our home or among our friends. And for many years, the boys we knew at TL kept silent about whatever they experienced or suspected. That silence speaks loudly of the shame and trauma that accompany molestation.

In 1990, Farm & Wilderness fired Jack Sloanaker after receiving a report that he had molested a camper in the 1970s. (According to an article in the *Valley News* of October 27, 1993, this was considered to be an "isolated incident" and was not reported to the authorities.[2]) Sloanaker had occupied a central place at Timberlake since 1953, first as a counselor and then as a director. He had inaugurated the counselor apprentice program and taught white water canoeing and campcraft. Generations of former campers had continued to rely on the campcraft skills he transmitted. As noted in chapter 3, many also remembered his extraordinary musical ability. These powerful and positive memories have since had to be placed in a new context.

In 1992, an eighteen-year-old boy told Marion Perkins, a director at Family Camp, which ran at the end of the summer, that Sloanaker had sexually abused him in 1988 when he was fourteen at a home across the street from the Farm & Wilderness camps on Woodward Reservoir and again, a year later, at Sloanaker's "secret place," a "lean-to campsite adjacent to Farm and Wilderness property in Mount Holly."[3] Because Perkins was a mandated reporter, she informed the Windsor County State Attorney General's office. In February 1994, Sloanaker pleaded no contest to "lewd and lascivious conduct with a child" as part of a plea agreement. He received a two- to five-year suspended sentence and was required to attend a sex offenders program, perform two hundred hours of community service, and refrain from contacting the victim and any child under the age of eighteen.[4]

While the plea deal was under review (as part of a presentencing investigation), the case took a new turn. Farm & Wilderness executive director Len Cadwallader visited John Bancroft, a former camper, during a recruiting trip to Seattle. Viewing photographs from Bancroft's time at F&W, Cadwallader mentioned that Sloanaker no longer worked there. "And just, without even thinking, I said, 'Oh, is it for child abuse by any chance?'" Bancroft told us. "And then he kind of startled."[5] Cadwallader suddenly realized that the problem was much larger than he previously had understood.

Bancroft wrote to the attorney general's office to report that Sloanaker had molested him in 1959. Soon afterward, the F&W Board sent a letter to eight thousand former campers informing them of the charges against Sloanaker and asking whether he had also sexually abused them at F&W. "That created," Cadwallader recalled, "an avalanche of letters." By March 1994, between fifteen and twenty people had replied that Sloanaker had abused either them or someone they knew.[6] According to the investigating police officer, the stories were remarkably similar: "The method was exactly the same . . . with only slight variations."[7]

In light of the new evidence, the attorney general's office rescinded the original deal. A June 30 hearing on a new plea deal attracted a sizable crowd. On the left sat two dozen of Sloanaker's supporters, including, according to the *Rutland Daily Herald*, "teachers, textbook writers, attorneys, book editors, artists, and musicians." One of those supporters, Rick Hausman, speaking to a reporter, gave high praise to Sloanaker and his influence at F&W: "Jack has so many facets to his life, and each of those facets have touched hundreds of people."[8] On the right were "the alleged victims and their families," who "were equally diverse in their professions and the number of miles they had to travel to attend the hearing." (As they entered, attendees asked one another which side of the room they should head to. When the Webbs' son, Robert, purportedly bellowed "there are not two sides here," a woman who had been molested by Sloanaker purportedly bellowed back, "Well, that's fine to say as long as someone pays my psychiatrist bills!"[9])

John Bancroft had arrived from Seattle, relying on the airfare paid by a brother of the survivor who brought the case to Marion Perkins. Bancroft's comments to the reporter were very different from those of Hausman, his former cabinmate: "I'm glad this criminal will be off the street. . . . I'm glad he's finally going to pay the price for what he's done." A man who had organized a survivors' group added that the sentencing offered the "opportunity for real closure for us. I'm glad now there is some resolution."[10] Speaking for the camps, Len Cadwallader praised the "victim-survivors and their courage for steps they've taken to break the silence."[11]

The judge sentenced Sloanaker to a year in jail. In addition, he was ordered to complete sex offender treatment, reimburse his victim $5,000 for counseling, "design a day-long course on the dangers of hubris, defined as excessive pride and arrogance, and the duty of leaders to exemplify the law," and "conduct 12 sessions free of charge throughout New England and upper New York state for public and private sector leaders" on that issue.[12]

Although the board's letter of 1994 had focused on Sloanaker, the replies alleged that four other counselors had molested campers. Moreover, unlike Sloanaker's actions, these alleged abuses had occurred on camp grounds. The board forwarded the names of those four men to the state police. The statute of limitations (the deadline for filing criminal claims), however, had passed, and the men could not be prosecuted. As a result, the names never were made public. Our interviewees disagreed about whether we should disclose them here. One survivor said that the men were criminals and that only complete transparency could rid Timberlake of its "illness." Others, however, were willing to leave the damage the counselors had inflicted in the past. Ultimately, we chose to comply with the request from the current executive director, Frances McLaughlin, and the Webbs' granddaughter Kristi Webb, who was clerk of the board when we spoke with her about this issue, that we not name anyone besides Jack Sloanaker. We also do not name the men with whom we spoke who told us of their experience of abuse at camp. The one exception is Bancroft, who alerted Len Cadwallader to the extent of Sloanaker's abuse and spoke openly to reporters.

Before we embarked on this study, we had heard stories about the sex abuse that had occurred at Timberlake. We were stunned, however, to discover how widespread it appears to have been and that it had probably been an issue at Flying Cloud as well. One man after another remarked to us, "Well, I was being groomed by so and so," or "I was abused by so and so," or "my brother / best friend was abused by somebody." Moreover, several former campers alleged that rather than firing the perpetrators, the leadership had transferred some to other positions at camp (as was the case for our brother's counselor). Some survivors we interviewed were among those who responded to the board's outreach by disclosing their own abuse at Timberlake; others had never shared that information with F&W.

As far as we can tell, Indian Brook offers a striking contrast. Although we asked many alumni whether they had heard rumors of abuse at IB, no one had. That may help explain why many women we interviewed remembered feeling completely safe there.[13] In our interviews, we also probed for occasions when counselors at Tamarack Farm took advantage of their teenage charges. We heard only one story of a male counselor touching, and eventually kissing, a female camper. When she made it clear that she wanted him to stay away from her, the harassment stopped. We have no way of knowing if additional occasions of any type of abuse occurred at any of the camps but were never disclosed.

RECOGNIZING CHILD SEXUAL ABUSE AS A SOCIAL PROBLEM

Because we found the reports about Timberlake so disturbing, we decided to try to place them in context. Most instances of molestation had occurred long before the public was aware that the sexual abuse of children was prevalent and harmful.[14] The 1962 publication of C. Henry Kempe's article "The Battered-Child Syndrome" brought the first media attention to the physical abuse of children and spurred the enactment of child abuse reporting laws.[15] Within ten years, most states had legislation requiring doctors, teachers, and certain other professionals (such as F&W staff member Marion Perkins) to report cases of suspected child abuse. In 1974, Congress passed the Child Abuse Prevention and Treatment Act, requiring states to adopt a uniform definition of child abuse to qualify for federal grants. Because the law specifically mentioned "sexual abuse" among the behaviors that constituted abuse, the number of reports of suspicious incidents dramatically increased.[16] Nevertheless, as late as 1978, Kempe defined child sexual abuse as a "hidden pediatric problem and a neglected area."[17] It is hardly surprising, then, that episodes of sexual abuse that occurred at Farm & Wilderness in the 1950s, 1960s, 1970s, and even 1980s were largely unnoticed or, if suspected, ignored.

Interest in child molestation mushroomed in the 1980s, largely as a result of allegations against the McMartin Preschool in Manhattan Beach, California. A Los Angeles grand jury indicted Rodney Buckey and six other teachers for molesting forty-eight children. Because the case ended without a single conviction, opinion spread that the case represented a witch hunt and that mass hysteria had swept the country.[18] During the same period, several celebrities, most notably Oprah Winfrey, began to disclose episodes of sexual abuse they had experienced as children. As media accounts encouraged more and more individuals to reveal past victimization, the notion of repressed memories increasingly came under challenge. The establishment of the False Memory Syndrome Foundation in 1992, the year F&W first reported an instance of sex abuse, signaled the growing skepticism surrounding child molestation and the backlash against child protective measures.[19]

Attitudes did not change for a decade. But then, in 2002, the *Boston Globe* published a pathbreaking series of articles detailing the cover-up of clergy sexual abuse by Cardinal Bernard Law in the Boston Archdiocese. Rather than removing priests known to have molested boys, Law had transferred them to other parishes. The series received the Pulitzer Award and made headlines throughout the world. One observer notes that the articles represented not only "a towering journalistic accomplishment" but also a "turning point in the history of child protection as the public finally saw the outlines of sex abuse in trusted institutions."[20] Investigations soon reported that the Catholic Church had followed the same pattern in countless other parishes. By 2019, approximately 6,800 U.S. Catholic priests had been charged with sexual abuse involving at least 19,000 children.[21]

The sex abuse scandal in the Boy Scouts of America (BSA), another organization charged with safeguarding the morals of the nation's youth, eclipsed that in the church. In 2004, the public learned that the group had for decades kept secret files, called the "perversion files," containing information about leaders alleged to have committed sex abuse. Instead of warning parents and boys and reporting the allegations to the police, the BSA had hidden the names and forced the accused leaders to resign; in some cases, they had been allowed to move to other troops.[22] In 2012, the Oregon Supreme Court ordered the organization to release some of the files. By 2020, more than fifty-two thousand people had filed sex abuse claims against the BSA; that year, the organization filed for Chapter 11 bankruptcy protection to resolve the lawsuits.[23] The following year, when the U.S. Bankruptcy Judge Laurie Selber Silverstein of Delaware approved the BSA's proposed reorganization plan to exit bankruptcy, many plaintiffs were irate.[24]

While those events unfolded, the media publicized cases of sexual abuse in various other institutions. The Penn State scandal garnered special attention. In 2012, Jerry Sandusky, the assistant coach for the university football team, was found guilty of sexually abusing boys over a fifteen-year period. Soon after Sandusky's arrest, three Penn State officials—including the president Graham Spanier, vice president Gary Schultz, and athletic director Tim Curley—were charged with perjury, obstruction of justice, and failure to report suspected child abuse. In 2017, all three were found guilty of misdemeanor charges of child endangerment.[25]

On June 6, 2012, two weeks before Sandusky's conviction, the *New York Times Magazine* contained an article titled "Prep-School Predators" about students' claims of sexual assault and abuse at Horace Mann, an elite New York City private school.[26] The author, Amos Kamil, had graduated from the school in 1982; with Sean Elder, he later published the book *Great Is the Truth: Secrecy, Scandal, and the Quest for Justice at the Horace Mann School*.[27] On March 25, 2013, a similar account appeared in the *New Yorker* by Marc Fisher, another alumnus as well as a *Washington Post* reporter.[28] Although the school refused to conduct an investigation, a study by a group of concerned alumni reported that twenty-two Horace Mann staff members—including a headmaster, coaches, teaches, chaplain, and a dean of guidance—had sexually abused sixty-four students between the 1960s and the 1990s. Several of those students had either committed suicide or attempted to do so. Others attributed drug abuse, broken relationships, and stunted careers to the abuse they had experienced at the school.[29]

Because Boy Scout councils own and operate hundreds of camps, many episodes of abuse occurred there.[30] Nevertheless, summer camps as a category did not receive specific attention until 2018, when CBS reported that at least 578 children had been abused at camps in the past fifty-five years. "That's probably just the tip of the iceberg," stated Jon Conte, an emeritus University of Washington professor who studied child abuse. He continued, "I think it's isolation from parents. It's out of a normal routine. Some kids are a little bit older and they're feeling more independent, and they may have a false sense of security."[31] In 2019, Crime Stoppers, a nonprofit organization seeking to end child abuse, reported that at least one thousand children had been abused at camps in the past five years; the group added that the figure undoubtedly was much larger.[32] According to *Psychology Today*, "Summer camp is an ideal place for abuses; in recent years, sexual abuse has occurred at Christian camps, publicly funded camps, Boy Scout camps, and even the camp run by the school President Obama's daughters attend."[33] Rick Hausman, still struggling to understand the events that had occurred thirty years before our interview, reminded us that "camps, just like boarding schools or other residential facilities, where there are lots of children and they stay there 24/7, are fertile grounds for people who want to abuse kids."[34] A *New York Times* article about two online chat rooms for self-identified pedophiles underscored Hausman's point. Both chat rooms discussed employment opportunities at summer camps. "Did anyone," one man asked, "know of girls' camps willing to hire adult males as counselors?" Meanwhile, elsewhere in cyberspace, the second group celebrated the news that one of their own had been offered a job leading a boys' cabin at a sleepaway camp. But participants in the conversation did not focus on the work. "Hope you see some naked boys in your cabin," a man calling himself PPC responded, adding, "and good luck while restraining yourself from doing anything."[35] Although we have no way to compare the incidence of sexual abuse at F&W with that at other camps, it is clear that the practice has been far more widespread than previously assumed.

COMMON ELEMENTS OF SEX ABUSE SCANDALS

Because we now know much more about sexual abuse in various institutions than we did when the F&W scandal came to light, we can understand many features of that scandal that seemed incomprehensible in the early 1990s.

What many people found most horrifying about the charges against Jack Sloanaker was that he had been such a charismatic figure at Timberlake for nearly four decades. To be sure, his magnetism did not affect everyone. One former camper, for example, said he "found Jack to be a peculiar and strange person who I kind of kept [my] distance from. He had a certain kind of vanity that didn't sit well with me."[36] An Indian Brook counselor who saw him on her days off said she always thought "there was something a little bit funny about him. He would sort of laugh at just about everything for no reason I could see."[37] Nevertheless, many people would agree with Martyne Stout, a former Indian Brook counselor, who remembered Sloanaker as "charismatic as all get out."[38]

Reports about abuse did not entirely tarnish Sloanaker's reputation among either the F&W community or his broader social network. District Court Judge Paul Hudson, who convened the hearing on Sloanaker's second plea deal, reported that more than forty letters had been filed on his behalf; according to the *Rutland Daily Herald*, the judge added that they were "the most impressive set of letters he'd ever seen written about any individual." After the hearing, supporters, including former F&W campers "encircled" Sloanaker, "hugging him."[39] After years of reflection, one ex-camper still chose to focus on Sloanaker's positive attributes: "I learned so much from Sloanaker. I learned about music. I learned about woodcraft. The guy was a fountain of interesting things for me. So to this day, certainly since the sexual stuff about him came to light, I wish there was some way to honor this guy for what he did in my life. Reports of Sloanaker's abuse cannot completely undo all the other wonderful things about Sloanaker, as far as I'm concerned."[40]

Sloanaker's charisma was not unusual among predators. An article about sexual abuse at Kanakuk Kamp, a prominent evangelical Christian camp near Branson, Missouri, begins, "The first thing you need to know about Pete Newman is that people loved him. . . . Girls wanted to date him, guys wanted to be him, and children wanted to follow him." The article continues, "Newman rose through the ranks from camp counselor to camp director. [The camp] sent him on the road to recruit campers and to raise money. According to former members of the camp community, parents would sometimes compete for a coveted honor—hosting Newman in their home." But he was also "a superpredator." On June 9, 2010, he pleaded guilty to seven counts of sexually abusing boys and received a sentence of two life terms. A prosecutor in the case estimated that his victims numbered in the "hundreds."[41]

After investigating sex abuse scandals at various institutions, Amos Kamil concluded that typical perpetrators were not "monster[s] lurking out there in the darkness" but rather "trusted figures who tended to hide in plain sight, making themselves conspicuous."[42] He described three Horace Mann molesters. Mark Wright, a football coach, was "a great guy. Funny, gregarious, everyone loved him. He had this aura of success around him." Johannes Somary, the head of the arts and music department, "was a legend on campus. With his wild hair and faraway gaze, a jacket and tie over his pot belly, [he] seemed almost a caricature of a brilliant maestro. The son of a famous Austrian-Swiss banker, he enjoyed a prominent international reputation, having guest-conducted numerous orchestras, including the Royal Philharmonic of London and the Vienna Philharmonic. The walls of Pforzheimer Hall at Horace Mann were lined with posters from his concerts." Ian Theodore "was for many years the multifaceted head of the arts department. The sculptor, athlete, philosopher, historian, thespian and naturalist." Kamil "loved him and simply couldn't square the accusations with the man [he] knew." Even more than a teacher and mentor, he was "like a family member." In fact, he almost became a family member when he asked Kamil's mother to marry him. Although she rejected his offer, the two remained close. Kamil even named his son "Abraham Theodore in his honor."[43]

Moreover, the techniques Sloanaker (and others at F&W) used to gain sexual access to children can be considered common examples of what we now call "grooming."[44] One is to single out certain children as special, bringing them gifts, taking them on trips or out for ice cream, and granting them unusual privileges.[45] According to a *Time Magazine* article, Kendall Kimber, a Boy Scout, "had been tapped for an elite Scouting group, the Order of the Arrow, so he didn't find it strange when his Scoutmaster offered to help him with a project he needed to complete to earn the honor. But Kimber says that when he arrived at the man's house, the Scoutmaster handed Kimber a *Playgirl* and asked the boy to perform oral sex on him. Kimber, terrified, did so."[46] A Timberlake ex-camper had never thought much about his relationship with Sloanaker until he became a public defender and read a report of a case of sexual abuse in which the victim had been "groomed."[47] This man never was molested, but he suddenly understood that Sloanaker's favoritism toward him represented a classic example of grooming. Although Sloanaker did not participate in the Indian Lore program at F&W, several men we spoke to alleged that other counselors used that activity to bestow special recognition on their victims.

Another tactic is to choose victims who are especially vulnerable. A Horace Mann alumnus told Kamil, "'Although there are a lot of rich kids at HM, the kids who were abused were mostly from families of modest means. . . . We were also mostly from families where either the parents were getting a divorce or one of the parents had just died or was in the hospital, or we were in serious conflict with our parents.'"[48] Five former Timberlake campers told us that Sloanaker's favorites included a boy whose father had suddenly died.

A number of other reasons can explain why episodes of abuse typically remained hidden for decades. We have noted that few people had heard of child sexual abuse before 1990. Rick Hausman recalled that "we didn't have the language" in the 1960s.[49] Ann Scattergood Fogg suggested similarly that she "wouldn't have probably recognized [Jack's predatory behavior] even if it hadn't been hidden."[50] Moreover, the sexual revolution had blurred some boundaries between appropriate and inappropriate behavior. As a result, Hausman added, there was a lot of "looking the other way or thinking that these things weren't a profound influence on people's lives." Although he reinterpreted some events in light of what he subsequently learned, he had not been able to identify them as abuse at the time. One man, who had worked at SAM, remembered thinking that "that's a different, strange, strange group of older people there" at TL and that "it just seemed like the cast of characters there was very different than the staff" at the other camps.[51] He also recalled that the reputation of one counselor at the TL waterfront dissuaded SAM campers and counselors from swimming there. They knew that if they went, they "would be stared at." Despite these observations, he had been unable to name his unease as an awareness of abuse.

Sloanaker's exalted status further hindered detection. Psychologists have noted the influence of the "halo effect," defined as "a cognitive bias in impression formation whereby the positive evaluation of one characteristic has a radiating effect on how other, non-related characteristics of the individual are evaluated."[52] Many people could not conceive of Sloanaker as a child molester because he continued to be so widely loved and admired. In a letter addressed to officials at the "Vermont Department of Corrections, Len Cadwallader, Executive Director, Farm & Wilderness Camps, Kenneth Kruckemeyer, Clerk of the Board of Trustees at F&W, and fellow victims of sexual abuse by Jack Sloanaker," John Bancroft illustrated this adulation. He wrote that before his abuse, "Jack had been my idol, the person I wished to be like when I grew up. The list of things he did which I had wished to copy was long: be a Campcraft Counselor, go to Harvard, be in the Navy ROTC, own a gun, a Swiss Army knife, wear Navy shirts, play the banjo, go bird-watching."[53]

And most survivors remain silent; just 25–33 percent report abuse in childhood.[54] Amos Kamil first learned about the Horace Mann sexual molestation ten years after he graduated, when he went on a camping and hiking trip with a few other alumni. Late at night, one man said that the football coach had sexually assaulted him and several others. "No one knew what to say, at least at first," Kamil wrote. "But then slowly, the rest of us started telling stories, too. One of the guys talked about a teacher who took him on a field trip, and then invited him into his bed in the hotel room they were sharing. Another told a story about a teacher who got him drunk and naked . . . Finally, we all went to sleep." Kamil continued, "Then we went home, and another 20 years slid by." Kamil did not think about that conversation until he learned about the Penn State scandal, thirty years after he had graduated from high school.[55] One former TL camper we interviewed said that he repressed his abuse until he was a doctor and attended a workshop on pedophilia. "Driving home from that seminar," he said, "all the memories came rushing back to me."[56] Another interviewee had responded to the 1994 F&W board letter asking about sexual abuse but then had told no one else about his experience until he met his current partner three years before our interview: "Even my life-long best friend; we've been best friends since seventh grade. I never shared this with him either."[57] Another survivor wrote, "For reasons which I do not fully understand, I did not report my molestation to Farm and Wilderness officials. I wanted to forget it happened, was ashamed, and wasn't sure I would be believed. Now that I know that Jack had continued to prey on boys for [over three decades] after he molested me, I wish I had said something sooner."

The silence around sexual abuse means that many cases came up against criminal statutes of limitation. In 1994, when F&W learned that the law prevented the prosecution of the four individuals named in response to the camps' query, that issue received little attention. After the 2002 *Boston Globe* articles brought it to the fore, child welfare advocates and others launched a campaign to amend the laws. They met vociferous opposition from many groups, including the Catholic Church and the insurance industry. Although most states have revised their laws to some extent, arbitrary deadlines continue to protect institutions from child sex abuse charges.[58]

Revelations of sexual abuse commonly generate efforts to try to understand institutional cultures that ignore, condone, or even facilitate it. When we asked ex-campers and staff how they would explain the sexual abuse at F&W, most focused first on the practice of nudity. "All the emphasis on nudity, you know, did attract a particular kind of person," Rick Hausman said. Another former Timberlake camper we interviewed was David Finkelhor, a leading authority on child victimization. Finkelhor noted that nudism could have facilitated abuse by making "the transition from something that is normal to something that is violative much easier.'"[59] Significantly, reforms instituted by both the Boy Scouts and some camps in response to sex abuse reports include prohibitions on skinny-dipping.[60]

Finkelhor also reminded us of another feature of F&W common to institutions in which abuse occurs: "Certainly in the Catholic Church, the Orthodox Jewish Community, and the Boys Scouts . . . it's we're special so we do things differently." As we have seen, Ken repeatedly pointed to the unique aspects of life at F&W. The belief in exceptionalism might have made campers unable to recognize when difference slid over into abuse. Asked why he thought people did not suspect Jack Sloanaker sooner, one man we interviewed, who was involved with the camps over a long period of time, remarked, "It just never crossed my mind that in someplace like Farm and Wilderness, you would have a director that was a pedophile, that just did not make a bit of sense."[61] Finkelhor added that glorification of F&W might also have made campers unwilling to "tarnish the reputation of all the good things" happening at the camps. Many survivors of abuse at F&W told us that they still cherished their memories of their time there and returned year after year. Many also had close friends and family members who spoke reverentially about the camps.

Our interviewees also pointed to the fluid nature of counselor/camper relationships. Adhering to the principles of progressive education, Ken Webb sought counselors who did not operate as authoritarian leaders. His 1948 article, "What Might the School Learn from Experience of the Camp?" argued, "A good summer camp does as important a job of education in two months as the average school in many more." The answer lay, at least in part, with "the qualities which characterize the camper-counselor relationship," which are "directness, mutual respect and liking, humor and humility. There is little pretense, no false dignity."[62] Bob Hausman recalled that as director of Flying Cloud, he looked for people "who could relate to children one-on-one and could, you know, sit down with a particular kid and not just teach them how to swim, but also how to listen to what it was like when their parents divorced."[63] Observers have focused on the role of intimate ties at other institutions as well. For example, a *Los Angeles Times* article about alleged sexual abuse by staff, faculty, and students at the Thacher School, an elite boarding school in Ojai, California, noted that it "encourages informal, familial relationships among students and teachers, most of whom live on campus, dine and camp together." The blurring of boundaries had left "youths susceptible to grooming by adults, unchecked harassment, and alleged rapes."[64]

Finally, the ex-campers and staff we spoke to pointed out that responsibility for protecting children at Farm & Wilderness rested with the camp leaders, including Ken Webb. One woman blamed "a devastating failure of leadership. Who hired Jack Sloanaker and didn't monitor even little tendrils of things that may have come through? . . . It is very difficult to understand how someone like that can do what they do for so long."[65] Neil Rolnick, a former Timberlake camper, said it took "a long stretch of the imagination to think that these men were abusing boys, and no one knew. The fact that this was happening, and no one was saying anything, to me means it's rotten at the top."[66] John Bancroft was equally blunt: "In my opinion, the camps share some responsibility for what Jack has been able to perpetrate on F&W campers. The camps put Jack in the positions of responsibility he was in for almost 40 years, often turning a blind eye to what should have been alarm bells that something was not right."[67] As we have seen, reports of sex abuse at different institutions similarly focus on those in power.

THE RESPONSE

Although the sexual abuse at the camps resembled that at many other institutions, F&W's response was very different—at least after the early nineties. One of the most shocking features of child abuse scandals in several institutions was the length to which the leaders went to cover them up. Studies of molestation in Boy Scout troops emphasize management's concealment of the so-called perversion files. Three Penn State officials were charged with failing to report suspected child abuse. The *Boston Globe* articles highlighted the role of Cardinal Law in camouflaging the abuse in the Catholic Church. And in 2022, the press reported that former Pope Benedict, then called Josef Ratzinger, denied any knowledge of the sex abuse that had occurred during his tenure as Archbishop of Munich between 1977 and 1982 although documents indicated that he had been present at meetings where the subject had been discussed.[68]

We have noted that our interviewees claimed that for many years, F&W reassigned Timberlake and Flying Cloud counselors who were alleged to have abused boys. When the reports became public in 1994, however, Cadwallader consulted a psychologist "who had experience dealing with predation" and who advocated that he act with complete transparency. As we have seen, the camps reported Sloanaker's actions to the attorney general, cooperated with the investigations, and tried to learn about the extent of the problem by canvassing as many former campers as possible. In addition, the camps were acutely aware of the survivors' pain. In recognition of that pain, Len Cadwallader told us he personally answered every letter from campers recounting their abuse.

John Bancroft found these efforts insufficient. In his letter of March 4, 1994, he wrote that he had not gotten much assistance "in helping deal with the damage Jack has done via his connection with the camps."[69] As in other cases of child sexual molestation, survivors reported serious mental health repercussions.[70] One wrote,

There were many consequences, some immediate and some long range which directly resulted from being molested by Jack. At about that time, I began having sleep problems, and at age 14 frequently had to take tranquilizers or sleeping pills to sleep. I also suffered from periodic depression. I became suspicious of male adults, and did not want to confide in them. . . . In general, I began to shy away from new school friendships with boys. . . . I was no longer able to confide or trust in most males.

I sought therapy in 1964, trying to deal with [a personal issue] and being molested by Jack. But I found myself unable to even mention the latter at that time. In 1975, I began to see a therapist . . . once a week for about two years. As we continued to explore my periodic depression and lack of ability to sustain relationships, more and more time was spent examining my relationship with Jack. This was the first time I told anyone about what Jack had done to me. . . .

I have seen therapists on numerous occasions since 1975. . . . I have had to spend a great deal of time (and money!) untangling my feelings about my molestation and the negative life patterns my experience with Jack led to.[71]

Learning about the abuse at Timberlake darkened our own memories of F&W and those of at least some of our peers. We looked back more critically at what one person called the almost "cultlike" experience, the mystique of the place, the belief that whatever we did at our camp was better than what kids did at other camps. We came to acknowledge our own participation in the idealization of F&W and learned to accept more complex, and occasionally very conflicted, feelings.

The scandal also severely damaged the camp's public reputation. Martyne Stout had been a camper at IB in the 1960s and returned as a staff member in 1975. She told us how difficult it had been for her twenty years later when she was teaching in a public school in central Vermont because this was "huge news, it was all over the *Burlington Free Press*," and people knew she was associated with F&W. According to Cadwallader, Timberlake's enrollment, "which had been very strong, just fell off the cliff."

In the years that followed, F&W implemented policies for hiring and training staff and for conducting interactions between staff and campers. We review these in the conclusion.

6 · RACE

Despite the attention lavished on the history of school desegregation, challenges to segregated recreation have just begun to receive attention. As historian Marcia Chatelain notes, "Camp civil rights movement activism involved many of the same aspects of parent protest for integrated schools: fundraising and institution building, determining whether integration or accommodation was more favorable, and selecting representative young people to secure victories in racially mixed settings."[1] Ken and Susan Webb were at the forefront of that movement. They were some of the first private camp directors to enroll African American children and frequently encouraged others to follow their lead. Their role is especially striking when set against the wider landscape—the limited camping opportunities for African Americans, the first timid attempts to enroll Black campers in previously all-White subsidized camps, the extreme reluctance of White private camps to admit any Black children, and the association of all interracial activities with communism after World War II. Because little is known about camp integration in general, we first explore these issues here.[2] We then discuss changes at F&W wrought by the social movements of the 1960s.

AFRICAN AMERICAN CAMPS

Overnight camps in the second half of the twentieth century took many forms, but three major types can be identified. Charitable camps, often associated with the Fresh Air Fund, served children deemed "underprivileged." Camps operated by national organizations such as the Boy Scouts, Girl Scouts, Camp Fire Girls, Young Men's Christian Association (YMCA), and Young Women's Christian Association (YWCA) enrolled middle-class and working-class youth. Those two types frequently are grouped together under the labels "subsidized," "organization," and "agency" camps.[3] Private camps like Farm & Wilderness had higher fees, newer equipment, longer camp sessions, and lower camper/counselor ratios than subsidized ones.

The first African American campers arrived at Farm & Wilderness in 1947 when, in Ken Webb's words, "we were asked . . . by one of the enrollment agencies if we would accept several fine Negro children whose parents could not find for them elsewhere the sort of varied camp offering they want."[4] It is not surprising that the enrollment agency could not find places for those children. As the *New York Times* reported in 1929, "Camps taking Negro children are few."[5] In 1944, the director of the Baltimore Department of Public Welfare noted the many camps for White children in the city "running all the way from subsidized camps for underprivileged children to fashionable camps for children from privileged areas where a substantial fee is levied." There were no urban camps, however, for Black children.[6] (In 1957, Farm & Wilderness had a brief exchange program with Atwater, the major private African American camp, established in 1921 on the shore of Lake Lashaway in Brookfield, Massachusetts.[7]) The overwhelming majority of African American children who had access to sleepaway camps attended subsidized ones. According to historian Brian McCammack, the camps established by Black branches of national organizations were "landscapes of hope that served as potent racial idylls: their remote locations, separate from whites, laid the foundations for race pride and dignity in ways that were difficult if not impossible in the city."[8] Many African American branches of national organizations, however, could not afford to establish camps. Until 1943, when a White philanthropist purchased property for a Boy Scout camp for African American troops in Paris, Texas, the members had camped overnight wherever they could, in pastures, woods, and designated camping grounds. Since 1920, White Scouts in Paris had attended Camp Clark on twenty-five acres.[9] Moreover, African Americans were not always allowed to form their own scouting chapters. Between 1933 and 1942, for example, the Nashville, Tennessee, Girl Scouts Council repeatedly rejected requests from an African American social worker to organize a separate troop.[10]

Finding a site for any kind of African American camp was a recurrent problem. Reviewing the first five years of Camp E. W. Young in Norfolk, Virginia, the city's African American newspaper, *New Journal and Guide*, wrote in 1951, "Handicapped by the baneful influence of segregation, the committee on camp site was hindered from the beginning. It was hard to find a place either in Princess Anne or Norfolk Counties or over the North Carolina line that could be purchased because of race prejudice."[11] After finally allowing African American troops to organize, the Nashville Girl Scout Council continued to obstruct their work. The council promised to buy land for a camp for Black scouts in 1947 but, in deference to the State of Tennessee Board of Parks, failed to follow through. Those problems were not unique to the South. In 1955, Darien, an affluent

Connecticut town, amended its zoning law in 1955 to block a Harlem church from constructing a weekend camp for African American children.[12]

There also was no guarantee that neighbors would accept Black campers after they arrived. In 1951, the *New Journal and Guide* reported that a guard at Seashore State Park in Princess Anne County, Virginia, "cursed and brandished a pistol at a group of colored children from a nearby church operated camp and chased them out of the park."[13] Four years later, twenty-seven teenage African American girls had to be evacuated from a camp near Versailles, Kentucky, after White men poured kerosene near the cabin. A farmer at an adjoining farm told police he had received a phone call that "some white men are coming down there to clean out the camp."[14]

CAMP INTEGRATION

One way to increase camping opportunities for African American children was to allow them to enroll in previously all-White camps. Private White camps, however, were even slower than other types to open their doors to Black campers. Ken Webb pointed out that the major impediment was the fear that "camp parents will object, that they will in fact withdraw their children and thus bring financial ruin to the camp." As late as 1961, he knew of only ten or fifteen interracial private camps.[15]

But subsidized camps also encountered numerous obstacles when they tried to integrate. Because recreation often involved close physical contact, it was more difficult to integrate than education.[16] Campers shared arts and crafts materials, sports equipment, canoes, and sleeping quarters. Sitting around campfires at night, some held hands and linked arms; at the end, they hugged.[17] Swimming, a central camp activity, was especially fraught. As historian Thomas J. Sugrue notes, "Whites clung to myths about disease, dirt, and black bodies, fearing contamination if they shared the same pools."[18]

Proposals to admit Black campers to all-White subsidized camps thus frequently sparked fierce debates and met resistance from parents. The archives of Henry Camp (operated by the Henry Street Settlement) contain numerous letters from White parents protesting the decision to enroll Black children.[19] When a Newark YMCA boys' camp accepted Black children in 1960, the enrollment dropped from 89 percent of capacity to 71 percent. The following year, the camp admitted children from the Fresh Air Fund, all of whom were African American, and enrollment fell further.[20] Some White parents who accepted integration in theory protested or removed their children when they learned that Black and White campers slept in the same tents or cabins or ate together.[21]

Integration advocates tried to assuage White fears in various ways. One was by arguing that Black campers and counselors received scrupulous vetting.

Harry Serotkin, a White social worker, wrote condescendingly that "the Negro counselor was an important factor in the success of inter-racial camping" at a previously all-White Pittsburgh YMCA camp. "A fine-looking, athletic and intelligent young man, he represented the finest type of Negro." The campers were "carefully selected Negro boys. . . . White and Negro boys alike came from good homes, had passed the same physical examination, and had interests common to intelligent boys of the same age."[22]

Directors also assured White parents that African American children would represent a tiny fraction of the camp population.[23] Ralph Roehm, the director of the New York YMCA Camp Custer, noted in 1945 that one way he persuaded White parents to endorse integration was to stress that "a few colored boys would not disrupt the camp."[24] Four years later, *The Atlanta Daily World* reported that the Presbyterian Synod of Baltimore "planned to limit participation of colored people at West Norringham camp this summer to a quota of 10 percent of any camp period and to three of the six-week camps."[25]

But even directors who recruited Black children exhibited some ambivalence about doing so. Most labeled their first interracial sessions "experiments," indicating that their commitment to racial equality was provisional and could be abandoned at any time. In addition, they defined integration in various ways, some of which we would not recognize as such. Some programs were labeled interracial because White and Black campers used the same facilities, though not at the same time. As Rev. James W. Asip, a member of the Brooklyn Interracial Council, protested that practice failed to teach children the "important art of living together."[26] A few camps that claimed to accept members of both races allowed White children to register first, often leaving no places for Black youth.[27] Other camps permitted White and Black children to engage in activities together during the day but then separated them at night.[28] Explaining the success of the interracial experiments at three Pennsylvania camps, Harry Serotkin pointed out that the directors "respected the wishes of those parents who wished their children not to be placed in tents or cabins with Negro children."[29]

Over time, most of these "experiments" were deemed successful. In May 1944, Serotkin wrote,

Five buses rolled towards the Pittsburgh Y.M.C.A.'s Camp Kon-O-Kwee last summer with 200 teenage boys singing gaily in them . . . Among the group were nineteen Negro boys registered through one of the Y's branches. Their presence represented the second successive year in which the camp was experimenting with a two-week inter-racial period. Eight Negro boys had come to camp the first year. The experience both years was the same. The Negro campers were made welcome and soon became a full part of camp life. White and Negro boys strolled together, hiked, planned, played, swam, shared tennis racquets together.[30]

Reports from both summers so impressed the YMCA's Board of Directors that "they unanimously voted to have inter-racial camping at Camp Kon-O-Kwee for the full summer" in the future.[31] A collection of celebrated photographs taken in the 1940s provides an image of racial harmony at summer camps. The African American photographer Gordon Parks was hired first by the Farm Security Administration, a New Deal agency, and then by the Office of War Information to document the lives of African Americans. In the summer of 1947, he took a remarkable set of photographs of children at interracial camps in New York State. Historian Amanda Martin-Hardin describes one of the most famous images, "Scene at the Swimming Dock": "The eye is first drawn to the figure in the top half of the image: a black teenager who helps a younger white boy climb a ladder out of the water and onto a dock. . . . The two figures are suspended in a moment of kinship, where the strength and virtue of the black boy are pivotal to the well-being of the white boy."[32] Some evidence suggests, however, that meaningful integration was more difficult to achieve. After investigating the camp operated by the Chicago Commons Settlement House, Marcia Chatelain concluded, "Young people would need more than a few weeks of camp to surmount deeply embedded racial attitudes, and black [campers] could do only so much to eradicate racism."[33]

Like African American camps, interracial ones also had to contend with hostility from the surrounding community. Some protests focused on swimming. In 1946, the *Cleveland Call and Post* reported that African American children attending a Salvation Army camp at Fort Herrick had been "taunted" while swimming at a local beach. When the camp bus had to be towed from the beach because neighbors put sand and water in the gas tank and carburetor, the director realized the only solution was to build a pool.[34]

Incidents in the South were more violent and destructive. Perhaps because Camp Aldersgate in Little Rock, Arkansas, hosted a mission school, a Black church, and civil rights conferences as well as a summer youth camp, it was especially vulnerable. During the conflict over the desegregation of the city's Central High School in 1957, the camp offered one of the few places where interracial groups could meet. At various times, board members and staff received phone threats; in addition, individuals fired shots into the campground and attempted to blow up the lake's dam with dynamite.[35]

THE RED SCARE

It is likely that the Webbs closely followed the experiences not only of subsidized camps but also of the camps established by Communist Party (CP) members, their allies, and other leftists. Since its prominent defense of the Scottsboro Boys (nine young Black men charged with raping a White woman in 1931), the CP had been at the forefront of the struggle for racial justice.[36] Coleman Young, later Detroit's first African American mayor explained, "The reality of the day was that anyone who took an active interest in the plight of Black people was naturally drawn to the Communist Party, not as a member necessarily, but at least as a friend and ally, owing to the fact the Communists historically had been out front in the struggle for civil rights."[37]

The situation changed dramatically after World War II. In 1947, the year Farm &Wilderness admitted its first Black campers, President Truman issued Executive Order 9835, requiring the investigation of the loyalty of all federal employees. In the same period, the nascent civil rights movement sought to sever its ties to communism. Civil rights advocates increasingly used Cold War rhetoric to advance their cause. Desegregation, they argued, could convince the world that democracy represented the superior form of government. Addressing the American Camp Association in 1952, the author Lillian Smith urged the integration of private camps because "minority group discrimination in this country is hurting the United States in its ideological war against communism."[38]

Nevertheless, communism remained intertwined with racial equality in the popular mind. The first attack on a so-called Commie camp focused on both. Camp Wo-Chi-Ca (a name that sounds Native American but is actually a contraction of Workers' Children's Camp) was established in New Jersey 1936. The highlight of every summer was the day singer Paul Robeson visited, and his name graced the sign on a large recreation hall visible to anyone entering the camp. After traveling to the Soviet Union in the late thirties, he delivered speeches comparing it favorably to the United States. In August 1949, mobs of White citizens attacked people attending Robeson's civil rights benefit concert in Peekskill, New York. Holding him responsible for the violence, authorities revoked his passport and banned him from giving public performances; record companies terminated his contracts. The following summer, local youths began driving onto Wo-Chi-Ca campgrounds demanding the removal of the sign with Robeson's name and threatening to burn the building down. When neighbors threatened to poison the water supply, armed staff began patrolling the grounds at night. In 1951, Wo-Chi-Ca merged with Camp Wyandot, another leftist, interracial camp, located in Mount Tremper, New York.[39]

Anticommunist hysteria targeted other left-oriented, integrated camps as well. On February 7, 1952, the *Baltimore Sun* reported, "The House Un-American Activities Committee today heard how the Communist party recruited members among New York youth through social and cultural activities and at summer camps." The speaker was Harvey M. Matuso, who had joined the CP but then became an FBI informer.[40] In 1955, the committee called directors and staff of various leftist camps to testify.[41] "Camps operated or influenced by subversive organizations or Communist fronts, no matter how few in number will be identified," Senator Bernard Tompkins, the committee chair, explained to the *New York Tribune*.[42]

F&W'S CHALLENGES

We cannot know to what extent Ken and Susan Webb assumed that F&W's association with Quakerism protected it from the red-baiting Communist camps experienced. It is at least possible, however, that the atmosphere of fear and repression in the immediate post–World War II era helps explain why they couched the need for integration in Cold War rhetoric. In his 1961 article, Ken wrote, "We find that in a humble way we can actually have some influence on the great issues which face the world; for it is becoming more evident every year that the east-west struggle is not going to be settled by bombs but by the judgment of the uncommitted 'neutralist' nations, *the great majority of whom are colored* . . . People in position to know what the real weapons are the Communists use against us with such devastating effect rejoice to know of every effort which robs the Communists of part of their arsenal."[43] The article continued with a passage from a 1948 letter to Ken from the best-selling author and social activist Dorothy Canfield Fisher:

> I think that I never had a letter which gave me more pleasure than your report of the result of your humane and civilized experiment in taking colored children in your camps. The pictures you sent are perfectly delightful and have been sent already to France, to friends of mine who write that they are under strong pressure from anti-American propaganda from Russian sources, one of the main arguments of which is that *all* Negroes are outrageously treated in the United States. I am busy collecting instances of American attempts to act in a civilized way on this subject, and your action has been one of my strongholds.[44]

But if the Webbs aligned themselves with the anticommunist crusade, they remained dedicated to social justice and refused to distance themselves from people who were attacked as communists. In *Beyond Our Wildest Dreams*, they discussed several. Two of the earliest F&W supporters were Owen and Eleanor Lattimore, who lived on Plymouth Pond (now known as Woodward Reservoir) in the summer, sent their son to camp, and provided financial assistance.[45] A prominent China scholar, Owen was accused of being a spy in 1950.

Recruitment trips to the South brought the Webbs in contact with civil rights leaders labeled subversive. They wrote, "Carl and Anne Braden, from Louisville Kentucky, who were leaders in the integration movement with Martin Luther King, Jr., offered their help when they discovered our interest in bringing black and white children together at Farm & Wilderness. They set up a chance for us to show Farm & Wilderness movies in their own home for their Black friends and one at the Unitarian Church."[46] Historian Diane McWhorter notes that "in 1954, the Bradens became the most notorious white people in the South by offering themselves as fronts for a black family to buy a house in an all-white neighborhood."[47] After the house was bombed, the Bradens were indicted for sedition. Carl Braden was convicted and sentenced to fifteen years in prison. His conviction was overturned in 1956, when the Bradens became leaders of the Southern Conference Educational Fund (SCEF), an organization established by New Deal liberals in 1938 and frequently red-baited in the 1950s.[48]

In Birmingham, the Webbs stayed at the home of Clifford Durr. "Clifford had been an official in Roosevelt's administration," they wrote, "and was widely known as a fearless liberal and a highly competent lawyer."[49] He served on the Federal Communications Commission (FCC) but resigned in 1948 in protest against President Harry Truman's Federal Loyalty Oath. Back in Montgomery, he reestablished a general law practice but lost most of his White clients in 1954 after the Senate Subcommittee on Internal Security called his wife, Virginia Foster Durr, to testify in hearings about the SCEF, led by Carl and Anne Braden.[50]

The Webbs had to contend not only with the association of integration with communism but also with the attitudes of the surrounding community. Vermont was virtually all White. An essay titled "Racial Elements" in the 1937 WPA *Guide to Vermont* focused on French Canadians and the Irish but made no mention of African Americans.[51] Because so few African Americans lived in or visited the state, there were few tacit or overt racial incidents. But some did occur in the years F&W recruited Black campers. The son of a freed slave, William John Anderson Jr. could not find a lodging room in either the Montpelier Tavern or the Pavilion Hotel after his election to the Vermont legislature in 1944.[52] In the late 1950s, the girlfriend of the University of Vermont's African American football star was refused lodging at a Burlington motel, and an African American air force captain assigned to the University of Vermont ROTC program was unable to obtain housing nearby.[53] Until 1968, the centerpiece of the University of Vermont's winter carnival included "two nights of elaborately choreographed skits by white students dressed as minstrels complete with blackface and kinky-haired wigs" as well as "simulations of slaves performing for masters, and students dressed in KKK and on one occasion a simulated lynching."[54] As Ken wrote in 1973, "Vermont has a reputation for friendship with black people, a reputation which, regrettably, is not always justified."[55]

Yet another problem the Webbs faced was the possibility of alienating their constituency, an especially critical issue for private camps dependent on fees. Chuck Meinhold, an early camper as well as a counselor, parent, and trustee for many years, later wrote to Ken expressing admiration for his decision to accept the first Black campers: "The camps were full for the first time and you were up to your neck in debt. We practical staff people said you just could not do this thing at the time because half of the camp was Southern and would leave . . . and you had a good out . . . the camps were 'full.' . . . I was impressed that you stood by your convictions even though it could have cost you the camps—and did cost you dearly when so many Southerners abandoned you."[56] Peg Espinola, an Indian Brook camper from Washington, DC, recalled that before her second year in 1947, her parents received a letter informing them that the Webbs had decided it was time to accept Black campers.[57] That summer, unlike Espinola's first summer, there were no special F&W cars on the train from Washington and Baltimore to White River Junction. She was led to believe that the cause was a decrease in the number of campers coming from these southern cities that year.

But Ken argued that his decision to accept Black campers had the advantage of helping him attract exactly the clientele he wanted. Although some southern parents had canceled their children's registrations in response to his letter, others sent their children "because the camps stood for the ideals they themselves believed in deeply. The degree of loyalty among the people attracted to the camps by this one action has been a joy ever since—and the true strength of the camps." Many parents also were eager to contribute to the funds set aside for scholarships "to assist campers who by reason of personality or differing economic status or racial group would give greater diversity to the camper group."[58]

Nevertheless, the Webbs were careful to alleviate any anxieties White parents might have. First, they emphasized the absence of conflict at other interracial camps. In 1949, two years after enrolling the first Black campers, Ken wrote in the *Nation* that he had "made inquiries at all the private camps and many of the institutional camps which I know take Negroes—the last assimilable group here in the East—and have not learned of a single difficulty in the relations of the campers." He quoted the annual report of another Quaker camp: "This year's camp, like the former ones, made clear once again that children are 'color-blind' unless prejudice is passed on to them from others. The children erected no barriers against each other on the basis of race. . . . Individuals were accepted as individuals. When campers arrived, they often had 'buddies' of the same race. Soon, however, new friendships were formed, and the color of the skin seemed of no consideration."[59]

Second, like directors of subsidized camps, Ken assured White parents that the Black children he admitted represented a tiny minority of the total camp population. His 1949 article continued, "Many an idealistic director who is also honest will admit that the interracial character of his camp would disappear if any one of the minority groups became dominant numerically. This paradox must be faced, and not infrequently members of the minority group are themselves concerned about the matter."[60] Observing a camp square dance twelve years later, Ken wrote, "Dark faces, both on the dance floor and in the orchestra, add variety and interest to the crowd."[61]

Third, the Webbs followed other directors in promising that they submitted Black campers to careful vetting. Asked by a *Christian Science Monitor* reporter in 1969 whether "inner-city Black children should attend predominantly white summer private camps," Susan Webb said yes but then added that "not just any inner-city boy or girl [can be] plunked down into any private summer camp." The article noted, "For more than 35 years, Ken and Susan Webb have visited the ghettos of Boston, New York, Baltimore, and Philadelphia to find Negro boys and girls who could benefit from a summer spent in the Vermont woods. . . . 'You have to do this,' says Mrs. Webb. 'You have got to be sure that your camp is the right camp for that child.'"[62]

One way the Webbs departed from subsidized camp directors was by asserting that the social backgrounds of most of the Black children admitted to F&W were as similar as possible to, if not occasionally more privileged than, those of the White campers. As we have seen, the Webbs frequently referred to their Black campers as being "fine." By this, they might well have meant that they came from homes that valued education or, better still, had achieved upper-middle-class status. White campers from the 1950s remembered that at least some of their Black peers attended private schools and participated in the elite activities of the Black community, such as the Jack and Jill clubs. One camper told us about a visit from a Black cabinmate who arrived at her home "with tons of suitcases . . . and with lots of outfits."

Speaking about the White parents, Ken explained in 1960 that those who could afford private camp fees also tended to be "educated" people who "realize there are Negro children of cultural and moral standards like their own [whom their] children should know. . . . But," he added, "they are completely unable to make the necessary contacts to bring about such association for their offspring. Consequently, they are deeply grateful when a camp in which they have confidence uses its professional resources to locate Negro children and to include them in a natural way in their groups."[63] Here Ken presented himself as offering a solution to a problem that residential and school segregation had created.

Ken and Susan's position received support from Gordon Allport's classic 1954 book, *The Nature of Prejudice*, which argued that individual biases could be lessened by "equal status contact" between Whites and African Americans pursuing "common goals."[64] The civil rights campaign launched by the American Friends Service Committee (AFSC) had long rested on a similar belief. From the beginning, the AFSC argued that interracial meetings were most successful when the members of different races occupied the same social status. In 1926, Rachel Davis DuBois, a Quaker activist who pioneered intercultural education, noted the "increasing demand for Friends and others to get acquainted with the race problems in America." The best way to accomplish this goal was for Friends "to make contact with Negroes of our own cultural level. The Negroes are making tremendous efforts to better their own conditions, and it would be a great help if Friends and others could come into closer association with them."[65] Twenty years later, Ken and Susan Webb believed that the best way to counter White prejudice was to encourage interactions between Whites and African Americans from similar backgrounds.

CAMPERS' PERSPECTIVES

Having selected a few Black campers who resembled the White ones as closely as possible, the Webbs adopted a color-blind policy. Peggy remembers only one incident that brought race to the fore. The wife and daughter of Luther Foster, president of the Tuskegee Institute (later Tuskegee University), were both at the camp in the mid-1950s, Vera as a staff member, Adrienne as a camper. At one point in the summer, Adrienne talked about having stones thrown at her when she rode her bike through town. When Peggy, from her White, middle-class naïveté asked why people did that, Adrienne simply explained race relations in the South. Peggy never forgot that conversation.

But most Whites who had been campers in the same period told us that silence typically surrounded the issue of race. Ann Scattergood Fogg, a camper in the early 1950s, spoke about Joan Cannady Countryman, who was one of the few Black campers in those years. She remarked that although Joan "was a very good friend," she "never once really thought about what it must have been like for her" to attend a predominantly White camp.[66] Berl Nussbaum, who first became a camper at Timberlake in 1958, noted that the year before he came to F&W, he had spent three weeks at a camp run by the Henry Street Settlement. "There I was really exposed to Black and Puerto Rican kids from much poorer environments," he said. "I remember getting on the bus and hearing kids talking about gangs and bullets. I basically was shitting in my pants for three weeks there. I was really scared."[67] At F&W, however, where Black campers came from households that were at least as privileged as his, he rarely noticed race. Asked specifically about race relations, Neil Rolnick, who started at TL around the same time as Berl, mentioned having worked alongside a Black cabinmate to achieve their Pioneer ratings. Now in their seventies, the two men still get together and talk "an awful lot" about race. But Rolnick has no memory of the issue "being foregrounded in my discussions and my relationship with [him] at all. We were just friends."[68] David Finkelhor, another TL camper in those years, used similar language. He recalled that Steve Simpson, an African American camper, had talked about "race a bit," but "it wasn't front and center in what was going on. And I think he probably realized that it would have been awkward at that time.'"[69] Janine Fay, a camper at IB at the same time, remembered the "only person of color" in her cabin though not any talk about race.[70]

Nevertheless, our interviews indicate that campers were aware of race, even if they did not discuss it. The White ex-campers we talked to had clear memories of the few Black campers they knew and the activities they shared. They also told us that, because they had little interaction with African Americans in the school year, they valued the experience of forming friendships across the racial divide. Two interviews suggest that, unsurprisingly, African American campers were especially conscious of race. Joan Cannady Countryman remarked that although she was aware that she was one of very few Black Indian Brook campers in the early 1950s, she could handle that because she was in a familiar situation: she had been the first Black student to attend Germantown Friends School. "I was the 'first' because I was the oldest—in third grade," she said to a reporter. When we asked Carol Rapaport Monteleoni what she remembered about race relations at Indian Brook in the same years, she told us a story reminding us that White and Black campers undoubtedly viewed some events very differently.[71] Her first boyfriend at camp had been African American. "I didn't really see this," she said, "but when my parents came up for a visiting day and saw me holding hands with him, and I introduced them, I thought everything was fine, but he said to me, 'I think your parents really didn't like me because I'm Black,' and I really hadn't picked that up. So either [that was] my insensitivity or his paranoia, who knows what it was."

If interactions at camp, as elsewhere in our inegalitarian society, inevitably were fraught with overtones of race, however, there were few, if any, overt conflicts or tensions. The Webbs emphasized the role Al Hicks played in fostering racial harmony. He had arrived at Farm & Wilderness in 1951 as a Fisk University undergraduate. "Engaged as a cook," they wrote, "Al came north for the first time, very uncertain as a Black man, about what he would find. His first surprise was to discover us waiting for him at the Rutland railroad station. He soon forgot his shyness and became part of the group when the counselors, needing another man, asked him to join their basketball team."[72] Except for his two years in the Army, Al continued to work at the camp every summer until his death in 1984. Susan added, "In the early 1960s a young man came to visit a girl he liked at the camp and wanted to stay on. He proved to be a real agitator, trying to organize protest groups. Al was a great help when I asked him what to do. I will never forget his quiet reply: 'We don't need this here. We live our belief in sharing the camps—all of us, Black and White together.' The agitator was asked to leave."[73] We will see, however, that by the early 1960s, it had become increasingly difficult to assume that Black and White campers always viewed themselves as being "together."

MOVING PAST THE LIBERAL NOTION OF RACIAL HARMONY

The tone of the civil rights struggle changed in the 1960s. Young activists organized a student group that was less conciliatory than the older generation of activists had been. The movement fractured as some Black people allied themselves with the growing Black Power movement, which demanded that African Americans concentrate on building separate institutions and expressing their own interests rather than relying on the more modest approach of the civil rights movement. Some also followed Malcolm X, a Nation of Islam minister who advocated armed resistance to White aggression. "I don't call it violence when it's self-defense," he stated. "I call it intelligence."[74] Regardless of their ideology, all oppositional groups faced increasingly brutal attacks.[75]

The Webbs' recruitment trips to the South thus exposed them to danger. On their first visit to Alabama in 1965, Mabel Hicks, the mother of the long-time Indian Brook cook Al Hicks, invited them for dinner with her family. "We parked the car in her driveway (it wasn't safe to leave it in the street with its Vermont license plate)," Susan wrote. She continued,

> It was a courageous act on Mabel's part even to have us there at this time. Ken noticed after everyone was seated, around the table, that Mabel pushed the bolt on the front door on the inside. "You have a New England license, haven't you?" she replied when Ken mentioned this. "A couple of weeks ago a car with a New England license was parked in front of a house where some sort of a gathering was going on. Somebody threw a bomb into the group. We knew who it was, but the police would do nothing about it. The times were very tense. We aren't going to have that happen again."

Upon reaching the Unitarian Church, they "found a blue-domed police car parked in front."[76] When Ken told architect and civil rights activist John Fuller, his host, that he "began to feel like an enemy infiltrating hostile territory," Fuller replied, "Right. You should feel it. We do, for we're marked as liberals in this way that's going on. . . . In fact, we don't think you should take that trip to Montgomery by yourselves. I'll drive behind you to see that nothing happens."[77] The trip was scheduled to take place a few weeks after "Bloody Sunday," when six hundred civil rights marchers had attempted to walk from Selma to Montgomery, Alabama. After local police had violently attacked them and blocked their way, the leaders successfully fought the case in court. The Webbs reached Montgomery at the same time as the marchers from Selma and heard them recount their police encounters.[78]

In Vermont as well, racial violence occurred. One incident became the subject of Howard Frank Mosher's novel, *A Stranger in the Kingdom*. On the night of July 19, 1968, shots were fired into the home of Reverend David Lee Johnson, an African American Baptist minister, three weeks after he had moved to Irasburg with his wife and children.[79] The same year, Governor Philip Hoff and Mayor John Lindsay of New York initiated the NY–VT Summer Youth Project designed to bring several hundred African American students to work and study with White high school students in six sites across the state. One poem sent to a local newspaper provides clear evidence of the possibility of hostility from some segments of the population. It ended with the verse, "But [Hoff] and Lindsay overlook one trifle, Every Vermonter owns a 30–30 rifle."[80] Susan was well aware of the controversy over the Hoff-Lindsay plan. In a letter to the *Rutland Daily Herald*, she wrote that she was distressed—but not surprised—to hear of the racism and negative response to the program: "I have discovered a good deal of this opposition in my work with the Church Women United. . . . Nevertheless," she continued, referring to the existing Fresh Air Fund programs that provided host families for children from urban areas, "Vermont has a long tradition of bringing Negro Children here." Susan indicated also that she and her husband would be discussing this issue with other Vermont camp directors. They would share their experience, including their conviction that "discriminating parents very much want this kind of broadening experience for their children," and therefore, "camps will not lose campers by taking such a stand." Nodding toward the developments of the 1960s, Susan, as a final note, pointed out that "socially engaged youth" might wonder why they are spending a summer in Vermont were it not for "the socially significant work in interracial understanding they will be doing."[81]

Perhaps because they had been so close to danger themselves and were aware of the hostility elsewhere in Vermont, the Webbs tried to make F&W a haven for activists' children. At Indian Brook, those included girls whose parents were at opposite ends of the movement—Donzaleigh Abernathy, the daughter of the civil rights leader Ralph Abernathy, and Qubilah and Attallah Shabazz, two daughters of Malcolm X. Years later, Donzaleigh Abernathy recounted her Farm & Wilderness experience. When she became seriously ill with appendicitis on the evening of July 4, the counselors took her first to the infirmary and then to the Rutland Hospital, where she underwent emergency surgery. "Thankfully," she wrote,

> I was never alone and felt so much love from my counselors and the medical staff, who attended to me until my Father arrived from his Civil Rights Campaign . . . and my Mother from our home in Atlanta. . . . I was only eleven years old, but I

didn't know how ill I had been. All I knew was that I wanted to return to camp, so I begged by parents and the doctors to allow me to spend the remainder of my summer at my beloved Farm and Wilderness in beautiful Vermont. Thankfully, everyone agreed. In my Abernathy Family we call the green hills of Vermont, 'God's country.' It is the place where I had become severely ill and was healed!![82]

Her father spoke equally positively about his reception in Vermont when he came to visit his daughter: "My trips to Vermont have led me to believe that it's a republic—nobody bothers anyone. It's not hostile here."[83]

When the two daughters of Malcolm X arrived at Indian Brook, the camp continued to follow its policy of de-emphasizing differences among campers. One former camper told us that she had shared a cabin with one of the Shabazz sisters and had assumed they had a lot in common because they both recently had lost their fathers. No one told her that her cabinmate's father had been a hero to many people and that he had been assassinated.[84]

Nevertheless, it was increasingly evident that the Webbs' ideal of color-blind camps never could be realized. Recognizing the desire for a separate space and special attention to their needs, Qubilah and Attallah Shabazz organized a hair salon for Black campers on the back porch of the Indian Brook lodge. (Although they received support from some counselors, others thought that they should be engaged in more traditional camp activities.) One camper remembered that by the early 1970s, there was a "critical mass of Black campers" and that the Black campers sat together and sang together (she added, "loudly"). At that point, she said, "Whiteness was not necessarily assumed." Still, she continued, she thinks it was challenging for Black kids to be at camp and that the staff was unprepared to deal with race. Mary Johnson (pseudonym), an African American camper who has had a long history with F&W, would probably concur. During her first year at IB in the late 1970s, she was walking with a group of her cabinmates and counselors when the occupants of a passing car hurled racial epithets at her. Her counselors, she told us, had no idea how to discuss this incident.[85]

In the 1970s, Indian Brook directors after Susan Webb struggled to respond to changing attitudes toward race. Although the camp now had a substantial number of Black campers, it had few Black staff. Black campers sometimes organized themselves into a separate group but at other times joined the activities of other campers. We were told that when Black campers asked to present a Black cultural program, one director worried that it would create discomfort. In the end, our informant said, the program was a success because it helped the White campers better understand Black identity and the reasons why Black campers needed to be by themselves as much as among White campers, even at camp.[86]

Whatever social and cultural gaps might have existed between the backgrounds of most White and the relatively few Black campers and counselors grew wider after 1978, when F&W established a relationship with SEIU local 1199. (The SEIU/Employer Child Care Corporation administered the Anne Shore Camp Program, which made arrangements for children between the ages of nine and fifteen to attend three-to-four-week sleepaway camps in the Northeast.) Between twenty-five and forty children arrived at F&W. Most came from racially marginalized groups.[87] Mary Ann Cadwallader, who occupied various staff positions at Indian Brook in the 1980s and 1990s, suggested that she now views the program with 1199 as a "kind of tokenism," very different from the Webbs' recruitment in the South.[88]

Although the directors tried to hire counselors who could better support the African American campers, they were largely unsuccessful. Mary Ann Cadwallader suggested that the low pay offered by the camp helped explain the difficulty of recruiting African American counselors. Other issues impeded efforts to attract middle-class Black campers similar to those who had attended the camps in the 1950s and 1960s. She remembered taking one couple on a tour of the camp. Although they had thought of sending their children there, the idea of "roughing it" had no appeal. The father said, "We don't know. We're a generation away from privies and we aren't so sure our kids need that." Other African American parents said they preferred to have their children learn skills like tennis at camp.

CONCLUSION

It must have taken enormous courage for Ken and Susan Webb to admit a few African American children to their previously all-White camps in 1947. The most widely heralded breakthrough that year was the decision of the Brooklyn Dodgers to field Jackie Robinson. Although eventually celebrated as the exemplar of a more enlightened America, he was regularly heckled by Whites.[89] The Webbs thus had reason to anticipate that some White families would refuse to send their children to an integrated camp. That year also witnessed President Truman signing Executive Order 9835, requiring that the loyalty of all federal employees be investigated and helping inaugurate the Red Scare. As hysteria mounted, the public increasingly associated all attempts to achieve racial equality with communism. Adhering to beliefs that were widespread at the time, Ken and Susan Webb, like the directors of subsidized camps, sought to promote integration by bringing together mostly White and a few Black campers from similar backgrounds. The Webbs' successors had to display a different kind of courage. African American campers who had been influenced by the Black Power movement had little interest in assimilating into a camp culture they perceived as White. As F&W's Black population became more diverse and more militant, the leadership had to find a way to address the needs of this new group of campers.

7 · SOCIAL CLASS

Ken and Susan Webb, like many other founders of private schools and camps, faced a contradiction. Although committed to social justice, they created an institution for the children of the elite. Most children who enrolled in camps attended subsidized ones. In 1958, the *New York Times* reported that 150,000 city children had left for camp: "Approximately 100,000 of the campers will occupy the 180 camps affiliated with such community agencies as settlement houses, the Boy and Girl Scouts, churches, and other groups interested in their welfare. The remainder, estimated at 50,000, will be enrolled in private camps from Maine to New Jersey."[1] Although most private camps kept the same campers throughout the summer in one eight-week session, the subsidized ones enrolled different groups every two weeks. We thus can assume that the disparity in the number of children going to the different kinds of camps was much greater than those statistics suggest. The folk music that permeated Farm & Wilderness glorified class struggle. The campers, however, represented an exclusive group.

Americans have long been more concerned with race than with social class. Despite the Welfare Rights Organization launched in 1966 and the Poor People's Campaign organized by Martin Luther King. Jr. and the Southern Christian Leadership Conference, two years later, the social movements of the 1950s and 1960s primarily sought to expand the civil rights of African Americans, not promote economic justice. It is therefore unsurprising that the Webbs said much less about social class than about race in their published writings. Nevertheless, they were aware that the camp fee was prohibitive to all but middle- and upper-middle-class families and tried to provide financial assistance when they could. Originally, on an ad hoc basis, they offered "camperships" to those unable to foot the entire bill themselves. A 1966 advertisement for F&W in the *Friends Journal* indicates both their willingness to support less privileged campers and their priorities: "The Outdoor Education Fund assures campers from varied backgrounds and all parts of the country. The Fund helps Quaker children especially."[2] After the Webbs transferred control of the camps to the nonprofit organization, the distribution of camperships became regularized with decisions made by a committee that included a member of the board.

CAMPERSHIPS

The Webbs and the subsequent directors might have hoped that because class can be concealed more easily than race, differences in wealth would not be noticed. For some campers whose families relied on financial assistance, that was indeed the case. A number of the campership recipients in the early years had parents who held jobs like university teaching, where they earned less than their professional peers; the parents of some other scholarship campers had low earnings because they had lost their previously high-status jobs when they were branded as communists by McCarthy. While these campers might have known they were on scholarship, they did not necessarily feel that they were essentially different from most other campers. One woman, quite certain that her parents had assistance her first year at camp, could not remember when, or even if, they had been able to pay for the full season when she started coming for eight weeks rather than only four. In any case, she always felt comfortable with her peers at F&W.[3] Peggy's husband concurred: although he knew he was on a campership, he thought nothing of it except that it meant he could go home after a month of homesickness rather than having to stay the entire summer.

Some scholarship campers experienced social class quite differently. One former camper, whose father was a psychiatrist, noticed income disparities when he first went to an informational session at the home of a wealthy family living in a Manhattan brownstone. Decades later, he still remembered "the big rooms [and] high ceilings" that were so different from his family's apartment in Queens.[4] He came to recognize that the "kids of greater wealth who went to private schools" were more "sophisticated" than he was, and although he was not "intimidated," he was attracted by a lifestyle that differed not only from his own but also from the one prescribed at camp.

Still, other campers receiving financial aid experienced something more than status envy. John Trent (pseudonym) was an eleven-year-old White boy from Upstate New York when he received a campership to attend Saltash Mountain Camp (SAM) in the early 1960s; he later worked at both TL and TF. He shared written materials with us (but asked that we not use their exact wording, his name, or identifying details). In one document, addressed to his colleagues at F&W, he wrote about his anxieties about being on a campership and his fear that he would not be able to return if he did not meet the expectations of his counselors. Trent also wrote that although he eventually found a home at F&W, he knew from personal experience that that was not the case for all campers relying on scholarships. During his interview, he discussed what he saw among other campers from low-income families, especially among those from rural Vermont when he was on the staff at TF: "It was rough for the really sort of hardscrabble . . . kids from Vermont to make it at Tamarack farm. . . . [It] was a tough change [for them]." F&W was "still a camp for entitled people, basically with some other people thrown in . . . so we could all say we had enough people of color [and] enough poor kids."⁵ (A colleague of Trent's from the same period similarly commented on how difficult it had been for farmers' children from Vermont to feel comfortable at F&W: "There was a big class difference. You have just some kid [who's] been living on a farm and why would they bond? They're just bewildered when they meet somebody from this rich suburb of whatever city."⁶)

Trent also spoke openly about how he felt when he first came to camp: "There was the sense of being other. I knew everybody else had money, and they paid to go and I didn't. And so you had that scholarship mentality where you better present yourself well." He believed that being physically gifted—"I was good at chopping wood and good at doing all the things that needed to be done"—helped ensure his acceptance. And, he explained, he also developed a personal coping strategy. The son of a woman who cleaned houses and a father who was a carpenter, he had grown up in a town that he described as "a very White, secluded environment with the really rich and then the serving class, and my folks were in the serving class. I had never to my knowledge met a Jewish person." At SAM, he handled his experience of difference in two ways. Having gone with his mother to clean houses, he was able to imitate her "subservient" demeanor and say very little. He also spent much of his time with an African American camper who also "was out of his element."

Gradually, however, Trent developed a strong sense of connection. He realized his world had opened up. "I think my mom understood this," he continued, "that I kind of found my people." When he returned to school in Upstate New York, he "carried around a little piece of me" that was new. "I knew about another world that a lot of these folks didn't know about. I wasn't about to mouth off about it a whole lot, but people who were close to me began to hear about it."

Unlike John Trent and the "hardscrabble kids" he remembered, a former IB camper, the daughter of a single mother and the recipient of a campership in the 1980s, said that from the beginning, she knew how to "pass" at F&W because she was a scholarship student at an elite New York City private school.⁷ She also noted that from her perspective (and as the Webbs undoubtedly hoped), the Quaker value of "simplicity" made class, unlike race, largely invisible.

All of these scholarship campers were White. Some had learned to hike and camp even before coming to F&W. Some, like the "hardscrabble" kids from rural Vermont, knew their way around the countryside. The campers who arrived when F&W began partnering with the Anne Shore Camp Program could not make an equally easy transition. They had to grapple with an entirely novel environment. They also had to contend with counselors who identified their campers' difficulties as stemming primarily from their being members of racially marginalized communities and who felt at a loss about how best to help them. Ann Scattergood Fogg, who had returned to work at IB as an adult with a young child, remembered "seeing children who were miserable and one of them that sticks in my mind was an African American child from New York who was plunked down in camp. She had never seen anything like that. She was frightened I think by the dark at night and by all the unfamiliar kinds of activities and things."[8] It was a time, Fogg continued, "when they were trying to get kids from the inner city to come. And sometimes it worked and sometimes it didn't. I don't think we knew how to do it." Martyne Stout, who had been a camper at IB in the 1960s and returned as a counselor in the 1970s, recalled a girl "from one of those unions or groups" who was terrified when she saw a chipmunk, mistaking it for a rat. Having been promised that camp would be different from her home in the city, the girl was enraged: "I didn't think there would be any rats here. They're rats in my building. There shouldn't be any rats here."[9] We were told that one of IB's directors, like Fogg and Stout, also elided the issues of class and race as she evaluated the Black cultural program in the 1970s. While the director wanted to retain IB's basic premises and values that had been set in place by Susan Webb, she recognized that changes would have to be made in both policies and expectations now that the camp was serving children whose parents were not professionals.

STAFF

To ease the financial burden of being at camp, F&W created half-work / half-camper positions for some teenagers. These generated their own moments of awkwardness and confusion. Mindy Thompson Fullilove first came to the camps as a baby-sitter each morning for a dance teacher's young daughter; she much preferred the afternoons when she "played with the other campers."[10] John Wilhelm was on a campership for his first month at Tamarack Farm in 1960. As the end of that time approached, Wilhelm told us, Jack Bailey (the director) "worked out this kind of hokey scheme that allowed me to stay where I was, supposedly earning my right to stay the second half of that summer by working in the tool shed in the morning."[11] For the next three summers, the directors continued to "cook up some kind of scheme" so he could continue to return, "which," he added, "was phenomenal." Three other interviewees also told us that they had "staff" positions even though they were the same ages, or even younger than some of the campers, and that they did not always know which group to join for social activities. One of these, a girl who babysat for a three-and-a-half-year-old when she was twelve, loved being at camp, although, she admitted, she couldn't handle the child she was supposed to care for during the day.[12] The following summer, she was thrilled to return as a regular camper, even though her family could only afford to send her for half the season (and her sister for the other half).

These betwixt and between positions paid nothing beyond the privilege of being at F&W for the summer. Of course "real" staff were paid, albeit not lavishly. One former camper remembered that in 1953, his older brother had received $50 for the entire summer (plus room and board, of course) as a junior counselor at TL, an amount that would be worth $544 today. Ten years later, when he held his own first job as a TL counselor, he said, the pay had "skyrocketed" to $200, equivalent to $1,898 today.[13] In 2021, summer staff salaries started at even less than that, at $1,200, and rose from there, according to number of years' experience, any extra skills or certifications, if they were at TF, and other factors. (The camp website describes a variety of paid employment positions but does not list current wages.) During the summer of 2022, according to ZipRecruiter, teen summer jobs paid between $6.49 and $27.64 an hour, with a national average of $18.[14] At that average rate, a teen could expect to earn $5,760 for full-time employment for eight weeks, far above the rates in 2021, even with room and board thrown in. Low pay might well make it difficult for F&W to attract an economically diverse staff.

Moreover, for much of its history, F&W often has had a decidedly elitist cast, especially with respect to college. Harvard, Ken's alma mater, was the ideal (at least for the boys). We recall that Tony Parkes said that many F&W people either went to Harvard or wanted others to think they went there. A cartoon in a 1953 *Thunderbird* depicted a figure in a mortarboard saying, "I just graduated from 'Hahvud,' and I'd just *love* to be a counselor at Timberlake." Four years later, Ken wrote in the same newspaper that "some people imply that you have to go to Harvard" to be a Timberlake counselor. He then enumerated "certain qualities and attitudes" prospective counselors should have but did not deny that a Harvard association could help. A counselor from the 1990s told us that she "always felt looked down upon because I wasn't from Brown or Cornell or alum of any of those schools."[15]

CONCLUSION

In recent years, F&W has found ways to further diversify the camper population. By the 2020s, the camps were regularly distributing as much as half a million dollars to approximately two hundred campers. Some of that was in Qualified Tuition Reduction (staff receive a percentage reduction in their children's fees) and some in outright requests to the fund. The admissions website urged parents to consider applying for support, noting that in 2021, the median family income for campership awards was $130,000 and that approximately half of all campers received financial assistance of some kind. A banner heading that page proudly announced that "every family who applied for financial aid in 2021 received an award!" In 2022, the camps launched a new program, called "Affordable for All." The website explains that F&W aims to be transparent about its financial aid, help more families through assistance for expenses beyond those of tuition alone, and in that way, remain true to the ideals of its founders: "At Farm & Wilderness diversity has been a matter of fact since our founding. Ken and Susan Webb, who opened Timberlake camp in 1939, sought to have our camps be inclusive and representative of the racial, ethnic *and socio-economic diversity* in our country." The campers on financial aid, like the early campership recipients, might find it relatively easy to make the adjustment from home to camp, particularly if their parents have professional or semiprofessional jobs. The case might be very different for those scholarship campers who come to F&W through partnerships the camps have developed in addition to the Anne Shore Sleep-Away Camp Program. These newer partnerships include the Saint Regis Mohawk Tribe Education Division (NY), the Vermont Migrant Education Program, and the Vermont Refugee Resettlement Program. Various combinations of race, ethnicity, and social class distinguish the campers who come through these programs from the rest of the F&W population. We assume that the greater understanding of different cultures among at least some segments of society makes today's staff—whether diverse or not—better equipped than previous ones to help such campers feel at home.

8 · INDIAN LORE

"Playing Indian is a persistent tradition in American culture," writes historian Philip J. Deloria. "It is, however, a tradition with limitations. Not surprisingly, these cling tightly to the contours of power."[1] By the time Farm & Wilderness opened in 1939, that activity had occupied a central role at summer camps for more than two decades. Incorporating elements from different tribes, camps erected tipis, totem poles, and sometimes whole villages. Weekly campfires, often called Indian circle rings, featured Indian stories, songs, prayers, and dancers. Campers painted their faces and dressed in beads, feathers, and fringed garments to stage elaborate dramatic performances.[2] Indian lore also pervaded F&W. The 1958 Timberlake program included "Indian craft, such as costumes, etc., body building, Indian games, archery, tracking dances, and Indian sign language."[3] Indian names were common: "wigwam" for a boy's cabin, "powwow" for a weekly camp meeting, "trading post" for a building housing hiking gear and food, "Indian safari," for a long wilderness hike, and "braves" for especially adventurous campers.

Then in 1965, F&W went even farther, establishing Flying Cloud, a new camp enabling a group of boys to live "like Indians" for eight weeks in the wilderness. A brochure from the late 1960s explained that "the culture of the Redmen, sensitively handled, offers much of deep value to boys brot up in the city."[4] Because the camp was based so closely on what were thought to be Native American traditions, it was especially vulnerable to charges of cultural appropriation. Long after F&W had begun to try to respond to Black criticisms of its "color-blind" policy, however, the Flying Cloud leadership ignored the many Native American activists who condemned the adoption of Indian practices and traditions by non-Indians.[5] Only after the turn of the twenty-first century did the directors slowly begin to jettison the trappings of Indian culture while trying to retain what they considered the camp's core values.

Like many other camp directors, Ken Webb had found inspiration in the writings of Ernest Thompson Seton, a naturalist who cofounded the Boy Scouts. Eager to find a way to deal with local boys who had vandalized his Connecticut

FIGURE 13. Scan of the cover art of *Thunderbird*, an F&W publication.

estate, Seton organized them into the "tribes" of the organization he called the Woodcraft Indians, told them stories about Indian lives, led them on excursions to the woods, set them to work making Indian costumes, taught them wilderness survival skills, and instituted a system whereby members could earn "coups," or honors, by completing certain challenges.[6] Seton recounted his experiences first in a series of articles in the *Ladies' Home Journal* in 1902 and then, the following year, in fictional form in *Two Little Savages: Being the Adventures of Two Boys Who Live as Indians and What They Learned*, filled with information about woodcraft. Seton's influence spread widely as he published additional instruction manuals, gave speeches, and visited many camps.[7] "The Red Man is the apostle of outdoor life," he declared. "His example and precept are what young America needs today above any other ethical teachings of which I have knowledge."[8] According to Bob and Rick Hausman, the first two Flying Cloud directors, Ken Webb frequently referred to Seton and used him as a model.

INDIAN GUIDES

A major way camp directors tried to lend authenticity to their Indian program was by hiring Native American guides. One of the most famous was Charles A. Eastman. Born in 1858, he was raised primarily by his Dakota grandmother until the age of fifteen, when he went to live with his father, converted to Christianity, changed his name from Ohiysea to Charles Eastman, and began his European American education. After graduating from Dartmouth College and Boston University's medical school, he worked as a doctor on an Indian reservation, advocated for Indian rights, and wrote nine books, including *Indian Boyhood, Indian Scout Talks: A Guide for Boy Scouts and Campfire Girls*, and *Chapters in the Autobiography of an Indian*. As a leading authority on Native American culture, he visited several camps in the Northeast before opening Oahe, a girls' camp, with his wife, in 1916.[9] "When Eastman donned an Indian headdress," Deloria writes, "he was connecting himself to his Dakota roots. But he was also—perhaps more compellingly—imitating non-Indian imitations of Indians."[10]

The first Indian guide at Farm & Wilderness also traversed two cultures. "Indian Lore with a real Indian" read the caption of a photograph in the 1940 Timberlake brochure, featuring a young man in a feathered headdress teaching crafts to five boys seated before a birch-bark tipi.[11] The "real Indian" was Wakio, known in English as William Rassenes (Bill) Cook. Born in 1922, he was a member of the St. Regis Akwesasne Mohawk nation, located on both the U.S. and Canadian sides of the St. Lawrence River.[12] The photograph had been taken at the Indian Village Wakio constructed south of Timberlake. A camper in 1941 provided the following description: "If you follow the Timberlake brook up the little valley beyond the pasture, you come to a lonely clearing at the beginning of the deep hemlock woods."[13] There you will find "the tipi, the Indian shelters, fireplaces, totem poles, etc. that go with an Indian Village. The bronzed form of Wakio, a Mohawk Indian, bends over the kettle where an Indian meal is cooking, or squats by the shelter where someone, sitting cross-legged, is working on a beaded moccasin or a feathered headdress." Campers can "spend whole days here, living as the Indians did, dressing as they did, and learning Indian games, dances, crafts." In the evening, "you will walk to the secret council ring to sing Indian songs and listen to Wakio's tall tales of his 'gran'pappy.'"[14]

Both Ken and Susan Webb described Wakio in reverential terms. Barry Wohl, a Flying Cloud codirector in the late sixties and early 1979, noted that Wakio fit Ken's "vision of the Noble Savage, who was filled with goodness and love of the land and ecology and fairness. It was kind of hero worship in the best sense, and I think it inspired Ken to be a better person."[15] The Webbs wrote that Wakio was "unspoiled," a term they frequently used to describe pristine, uninhabited wilderness. Here it implied that Euro-American civilization had not corrupted Wakio's innate virtue. They recalled that Wakio first arrived at F&W "as a boy of seventeen, fresh from the Mohawk Reservation." Because he was "well-schooled in Indian lore" and "took great pride in his heritage," he was able "to make this heritage live in the imagination of several generations of Timberlake boys." He taught the campers "to follow a trail he had laid through the woods and up the craggy heights of the pinnacle." The stories he told them "had been handed down from the tribes which became the Six Nations."[16]

Wakio impressed the Webbs for another reason as well. Although he was unaccustomed "to the customs of the white man when he first came," they wrote, "He had a rare quality, ambition." They then explained how Wakio fulfilled that ambition: "He had heard that Dartmouth still had scholarships for Indians, and he was determined to qualify. Many an afternoon during rest hour in his first two summers we sat on the hillside above the old barns and struggled with Latin gerunds. The miracle is that coming from such a different background, Wakio's unswerving determination carried him through the Dartmouth entrance exams, including Latin, for which he could get no help on the Reservation."[17] The Webbs here nod to their small role in helping Wakio while giving him the bulk of the credit for being able to make the leap from an impoverished reservation to an elite university.

During World War II, Wakio married Evelyn Kawennaien Montour, a Canadian Mohawk woman, and served as a fighter pilot. The letter he sent Ken in June 1944 reveals his close connection to Timberlake, even after he left. "Everything has gone well with me since my last writing," he began.

As you know, I am now in the Marine night fighters, and am now in the process of grooming my iron eagle and myself for our debut in the Pacific. We weigh anchor in the middle of next month, and we all look forward to it, as we have since we first soloed our Piper "cubs." . . . In the early part of next month, I am embarking on my final navigation flight; an eight-hundred nautical mile to land at the airport at Massena, New York. I have a refueling stop scheduled at Schenectady, New York, so I may be able to drop over to give Timberlake one good last one-over from the air in the first week or so—if visibility conditions are favorable. It will be in the first week or so.

He added that he was pleased that in his absence another Mohawk man would reside at Timberlake and that "the Indian Village will again be smoking with activity."[18] After leaving the military, Wakio enrolled in Dartmouth. "During his summer breaks from Dartmouth College," his grandson Tsiorasa Barreiro wrote, "he made presentations about Mohawk traditions at many schools, summer camps, and in performances, using his stage name of Flying Cloud. . . . It was part of my grandfather's drive to educate people about who we really are and move away from the stereotypes. He brought that education, vigor, and enthusiasm for native crafts, stories, and lore that Farm and Wilderness really took ahold of."[19]

Although the Webbs asserted that Wakio transmitted the lore that had been passed down through the generations, the reality was more complicated. Wakio's youngest daughter, Katsi Cook, told an interviewer, "I grew up in a traditional family deeply rooted in historical narratives, political action, and cultural memory."[20] Katsi's father died when she was nine months old. Her mother was sick throughout much of Katsi's childhood and died when she was eleven. Katsi thus spent much of her youth with Wakio's mother, a midwife. Nevertheless, the lives of most contemporary Indians differed greatly from those of their ancestors, and Katsi acknowledged that she had much to learn about Indigenous culture.[21]

Seton's writings appear to have been one source of information for Wakio. A description of the Indian Village in a 1941 *Thunderbird* noted that Wakio organized the camps with a "system of 'coups' for the achievement of various types. Those coups are based roughly on the organization of [Seton's] Woodcraft League."[22] Ken's 1973 book, *As Sparks Fly Upward*, described Wakio reading Seton's *Two Little Savages* to a group of campers.[23]

Ray Fadden may have been another important influence. The son of a Mohawk mother and a non-Native father, Fadden began teaching sixth grade at the St. Regis Mohawk School in 1938.[24] According to Katsi Cook, Fadden "was a teacher and . . . he taught both my father's generation and, through them, our generation, and gave us a great consciousness of just what it meant to be a Mohawk. He was an antidote to the colonial pressures of assimilation, reminding us that who we are and what we know has great value."[25]

It also is possible that Wakio attended one of the many Indian counselor training programs that existed. In 1931, *The Bacone Indian*, the newspaper of Bacone College, a Christian junior college for Indians in Oklahoma, reported, "Fourteen members of the camp counselor club succeeded in obtaining camp positions during the summer. Practically all of the [counselors] were in the East where the Indian is still a legendary figure."[26] The students had received positions with the help of Rev. William Brewster Humphrey, the executive director of the American Indian League, established by White Americans in 1910 to support Indian culture.[27] Wakio could have attended a program closer to home. In 1935, the National Youth Administration, a New Deal agency, began to offer one-week courses to Native Americans who wanted to be "Indian counselors."[28] Five years later, the *Rochester Democrat and Chronicle* reported that the program had produced a group of "young Indian braves and girls ready to take positions as counselors with various camps throughout the state to teach Indian lore to all classes of boys and girls. Some will go to Boy Scout, 4-H, military, private, and other types of camps where boys and girls desire to learn more about Indian crafts and camping."[29]

The Indian Counselor Handbook produced and distributed by the New York State Youth Administration enables us to glimpse the content of the education that students received. The author was Ellsworth Jaeger, a White man born in Buffalo in 1897. A prolific author and wildlife illustrator, he worked as a curator at the Buffalo Museum of Science. He also was a follower of Ernest Thompson Seton from a young age and later became one of his business partners.[30] Although the handbook included stories, songs, and plays, most pages contained extremely detailed instructions with accompanying drawings to help Native Americans pose as experts on arts and crafts from a distant time and place. He hoped that "for the good of both Red and White folk, these things shall not be forgotten and that many young people of the reservations will realize before it is too late that the culture of their forefathers is an important contribution to modern life."[31]

Because Jaeger had developed a close association with the Iroquois of western New York, he drew most heavily on their traditions. But he also included information about how to make Navajo fires, Ojibway "moccasins of long ago," and a Hopi shirt. The few descriptions we have of Wakio's teachings suggest that they too were a mélange. Wild West shows and the photographs of George Catlin had convinced many Whites that the Lakota, Crow, Cheyenne, and other nations of the Great Plains represented all Native Americans. The tipi Wakio constructed and the system of "coups" he organized belonged not to his own, ancestral, Mohawk traditions but rather to those of Plains Native Americans. Totem poles are associated with Native Americans of the Northwest.[32]

AFTER WAKIO

When the Korean War broke out, Wakio was recalled by the military. In 1952, he was killed in North Carolina teaching a cadet how to fly one of the first jets.[33] Nevertheless, campers continued to visit the Indian Village he had established, and camp advertisements continued to promise "Indian lore" along with hiking, canoeing, swimming, archery, and sports for many years. In 1967, Susan wrote in the *Lightning Bug*, "Linda Redmond, the Indian counselor, has put up her Cheyenne costume on the wall [upstairs in the main lodge] in the hope that you will want to make parts of a costume and maybe someone will get started on a whole one. It is a beautiful work."

The Indian lore program was especially prominent at Timberlake. For many years, the director was Bob Cochran, a White man whose Indian expertise stemmed primarily from his Boy Scout experience. In 1958, he wrote that he had founded "the Wau-Ban See Tribe, an honorary society of those fellows who showed the most interest and worked the hardest in the Indian lore program. Ten fellows were tapped out at two very impressive ceremonies, which were also enjoyed by a number of interested parents. These fellows were then subjected to a fairly strenuous ordeal, which incidentally, opened a new campsite to use which will really be a fine area after a bit more work."[34] Cochran based the program on the Order of the Arrow, a Boy Scout honor society established in 1915. Members dressed in "Indian" clothing and participated in "Indian" dances and ceremonies. At a "tap out" ceremony, successful candidates received three taps on their shoulders; they then underwent an ordeal.[35] Cochran had joined the Boy Scouts at thirteen and later been inducted into the society. Now he was a member of its board of directors as well as a scoutmaster.

We spoke to four men Cochran had selected when they were campers at Timberlake. Barry Wohl said that he had been most attracted by the opportunity of an "outdoor wilderness experience." The "Indian stuff" was just an "add-on."[36] John Bancroft also had shown little interest in the Indian program.[37] He remembered the induction ceremony well. At an all-camp event, "Bob Cochran himself slammed me on one shoulder and then slammed me on both kind of hard. And then you are tapped out . . . But my question even back then is why me, why us? We all showed zero interest in Indian Lore. And I'm surprised we didn't say thanks but no thanks. We thought the whole thing was hokey. In retrospect I'd say suspicious." Still another man told us that his father found "inappropriate" the "very phallic looking . . . symbol of special membership" (with its bear claw and ceremonial spears) he had received in the tap-out ceremony.[38] Like Bancroft, Berl Nussbaum wondered why he had been singled out. "The tapping ceremony recognized certain kids. I don't think there were any criteria for why that happened. I certainly don't remember us being more interested in Indian lore [than others], who didn't get tapped out."[39] Later, when he heard stories about sexual abuse at the encampment, he wondered if he had been "prey."

At least in retrospect, however, Nussbaum appreciated the ordeal he had undergone: "We were blindfolded and led off to someplace. It couldn't have been terribly far from camp because we heard bells, but it was a day of hard work and very, very little food. It wasn't like fasting on Yom Kippur, which would be a total fast, but we were working very hard and we went out one morning and we didn't come back until the following morning. That was a very, very valuable experience for me. I liked it a lot." When asked to elaborate, he said, "I never went without food like that. I mean, it wasn't totally without food. I think maybe they had a piece of bread for lunch or something like that, but boy was I hungry the next morning. The oatmeal I had is still memorable to me. I think it's very, very valuable for people to experience hunger and that was the most hungry I ever experienced in my whole life. It was in the context of camp, and it was in the context of Indian lore. So I thought that was a big positive." He also remembered the delight of dispensing with most of his clothes: "Running around in a loincloth was just wonderful, by the way. I mean, there's nothing as easy . . . as strapping on a loincloth, you have a little piece of twine and a cloth, and then you ran around and that was wonderful; you were barefoot to begin with. I loved that stuff."

FLYING CLOUD

In 1964, Timberlake operated a four-week Indian encampment for boys led by Arthur Einhorn, an anthropologist.[40] The following year, a new Farm & Wilderness advertisement appeared, offering yet another "Chance to Live like Indians." The fifth F&W camp, Flying Cloud, named in honor of Wakio (or at least of his "stage name") opened that summer. The campers wore loincloths, lived in tipis consisting of a tripod and seventeen poles covered in canvas, and engaged in various ceremonies.[41] Years later, the naming ceremony one camper attended remained vivid in his memory. Kenneth M. Kline, a freelance journalist, had gone to Flying Cloud in 1974 because he was "eager to learn about the Native-American blood that flowed in my African American veins, courtesy of both my grandmothers." He was not disappointed: "I'd been at the camp for two weeks when Medicine Rainbow, the camp director, announced that we would begin our first naming ceremony of the summer at that night's powwow. In the tradition of the Lakota Sioux, those selected for the naming quest would trek into the wilderness and spend three days in strict silence at a place called Blue Ledges on the edge of a mountain. There we would meditate on the names we had been given and how they would shape our lives." The ceremony began with a large bonfire. Soon, a camper named Running Bull Thunder arrived, holding a long Indian pipe. He was accompanied by four other campers in ceremonial outfits, complete with ankle bells that rang when they walked. Running Bull Thunder "offered a ritual in gratitude to Mother Earth and the Four Winds." When he took a seat, a drum began to beat softly. That "was our signal to begin the pow-wow, our late-night dance around the campfire, singing traditional songs. When the drumming stopped, one member of the group broke away. This was 'Stalker,'" who "walked lightly to the fire and unrolled a red quilt with Native American designs." He then selected ten campers, one of whom was Kline. Seated on a quilt, Kline held his breath as "Stalker came up behind me and daubed red paint on my temples." Kline then learned that his new name was Good Path Elk.[42]

Two counselors who claimed Native American ancestry lent the camp a patina of authenticity. Frank Standing High arrived soon after the camp opened and returned every summer until 1972. He presented himself initially as half and then as a quarter Lakota; later, he acknowledged that he had no Native American ancestry.[43] Born Francesco Salvator Vaccaro in Passaic, New Jersey, in 1934, he obtained a degree in fine arts from the Rochester Institute of Technology.[44] A hobbyist, he acquired his knowledge not only from books but also from two Native Americans living in the Lake George area. Because he identified as Lakota, he transmitted Lakota traditions. Jane Elkington Wohl had been a member of the Flying Cloud staff during Standing High's tenure. (Although all the campers were boys, Jane was Barry Wohl's wife and codirector with him.) Thirty years later, she wrote a paper titled "Reflections on Racism at Flying Cloud in the Years '68, '69, '71, '72, and '73." She recalled that Standing High "brought the 'Indian' mystique to FC with his braids, and his exquisite craft work that he taught to everyone who wanted to learn." But "he was in an interesting position and one that would probably not be tolerated today. After his first summer, he was not a tipi counselor. He refused to go on hikes. He smoked in his tipi (though not around kids)."[45] Moreover, his views on some issues clashed with those that were dominant at Farm & Wilderness. "One of the memorable conflicts of the summer of 1967 was over whether or not to fly the US flag at the big Pow Wow. . . . At traditional Native Pow Wows the American flag is always flown and always honored with a Flag Song. Standing High (who had served in the military as many Native people do) and [the current director] who was strongly against the US presence in Vietnam fought intensely over whether or not the flag should be flown. This was clearly a conflict of cultures on many levels."[46]

The next Native American counselor was Allen Flying By, a Hunkpapa Lakota from Standing Rock Reservation in South Dakota, who worked at the camp between 1986 and 1990. Sunshine Mathon, a camper at the time, recalled that he "renamed a lot of ceremonies and rooted them in Lakota tradition. For example, what had been the sweat lodge now became the Inipi. What had been the naming ceremony became the Wachipi. He led pipe ceremonies at the beginning and the end of camp and taught us a couple of songs."[47] But, Mathon continued, "when we marched in singing the flag song and marched around the fire at the beginning of the Wachipi, Allen was not there. He did not actually participate. In fact, he was not even in the firelight. Sometimes you could see him in the woods kind of standing way back." In retrospect, Mathon was convinced that "it was a deeply difficult time for Allen to both on the one hand have his traditions honored and cherished and, on the other hand, taken advantage of by a bunch of

White boys running around singing the flag song using the Lakota language . . . There was a level of discomfort or not knowing how to line up his real Lakota life and his real Lakota traditions and our effort at trying to bring some level of spirituality to our work."[48]

Flying Cloud also sought to attract Native American children. Jane Wohl remembered four from the late 1960s and early 1970s. After one of the first two developed viral pneumonia, the parents arrived one night and, under the cover of darkness, took him and his brother home. Two others came from Southwest tribes with a counselor who was a student at Arizona State. The twelve-year-old Pima boy "was tiny and apparently undernourished"; a Havasupai boy was more energetic and thus better able to participate in camp activities. "The questions no one was asking at the time," Jane Wohl wrote, "were why are we bringing these kids to FC? What are we giving them? Are we exploiting them using them as tokens? What are we implicitly asking them to do? Are we doing anything for them besides confusing them?" She found it hard to imagine "what it must have been like for the Pima boy to go home and try to explain what he had done for summer, and to tell his family that kids actually paid money to live without plumbing since in all likelihood, the poverty of his reservation meant that a great many people there were without plumbing." Jane Wohl concluded that "while many of our white, upper-middle class campers may never have met a Native American person, is it fair to ask a shy 12-year-old from the other side of the country to act as exhibit A."[49]

Nate Hausman expressed similar concerns about the Native American campers who attended Flying Cloud three decades later.[50] The nephew of Bob Hausman, the first Flying Cloud director, and son of Rick Hausman, the second, Nate had his own long history at Farm & Wilderness. He was a Timberlake camper from 1990 to 1991, a Flying Cloud camper from 1992 to 1995, a Flying Cloud staff member between 1999 and 2003, and a codirector from 2004 to 2006. He recalled that Flying Cloud made a "concerted effort" to recruit Abenaki campers in the 2000s and that his family contributed to a special scholarship fund for them. Although some Abenaki children probably had "meaningful camp experiences," Nate Hausman emphasized that Flying Cloud was a "challenging place" for them, "perhaps because of Native cultural appropriation issues and perhaps because of the broader F&W milieu that was so far removed from their experience and comfort zone." He doubted that any Abenaki children ever felt at home at Flying Cloud, and he could think of none who returned for multiple summers.[51]

We can surmise that the founders and early leaders of Flying Cloud viewed themselves not only as adopting customs and rituals that could have special significance for adolescent boys but also as protesting assimilation policies. In 1989, the Webbs wrote, "Native Americans knew the importance of rituals and ceremonies which can be useful to bind a group together and mark the passage of time. Our culture has discarded many rituals in a mad rush to 'homogenize.'"[52] Soon after Deb Haaland's appointment as secretary of the U.S. Department of the Interior (and the first Native American in a cabinet position) in 2021, she reminded Americans of the horrors of compulsory assimilation: "Over nearly 100 years, tens of thousands of Indigenous children were taken from their communities and forced into scores of boarding schools run by religious institutions and the U.S. government. Some studies suggest that by 1926, nearly 83 percent of Native American school-age children were in the system. Many children were doused with DDT upon arrival, and as their coerced re-education got underway, they endured physical abuse for speaking their tribal languages or practicing traditions that didn't fit into what the government believed was the American Ideal." Like many other Native Americans, Haaland could point to her own family's history: "My great-grandfather was taken to Carlisle Indian School in Pennsylvania. Its founder coined the phrase 'kill the Indian, and save the man,' which genuinely reflects the influences that framed those policies at the time. . . . We have a generation of lost or injured children who are now the lost or injured aunts, uncles, parents, and grandparents of those who live today."[53]

The Indian Reorganization Act of 1934 (also known as the Wheeler-Howard Act or the "Indian New Deal") reversed assimilation policies and granted Indian tribes unprecedented autonomy. Between 1953 and 1968, however, Congress passed a series of laws reinstating the goal of assimilation. The American Friends Service Committee protested the 1953 Indian Termination Act, which sought to force Indians off their reservations and into urban areas.[54] In 1969, Ken wrote, "No race was finer, more imbued with lofty ideals than the Indians at their best; that is, before they were corrupted and their culture was destroyed by the white man."[55] Four years later, he described the comments of Wakio's daughter, then a Farm & Wilderness camper, at a current events meeting. The girl "pulled aside the curtain of graciousness which was her usual personality, and disclosed an ugly depth of resentment, almost hatred, of missionaries, past and present, to her people. These missionaries, she said, had no understanding of Indian culture, nor did they *want* to see anything fine about it. They were bent on stamping it out to substitute their own misunderstanding of Christianity. They succeeded in robbing the Indian of his culture, his self-respect, his purpose in life; they substituted—nothing." Ken then commented, "Such words from people one knows and loves are deeply moving, confusing at first, until one's further search begins to give perspective. Then it can be ever more moving as it begins to crystalize a determination to do what one can to right some of these ancient wrongs."[56] Although we cannot know whether the girl ever made such a speech or even had those thoughts, we can understand the use Ken made of it. By choosing to focus exclusively on the missionaries out of all the White groups who devastated Indian nations, he implied that both the teaching of Indian lore at Timberlake and the establishment of Flying Cloud represented a tribute to the girl's people and a way to "right some of these ancient wrongs."

By the early 1970s, however, Native Americans had begun to criticize the use of elements of their culture by people from different backgrounds. Although the notion of cultural appropriation did not emerge until the 1990s, Native Americans listed several practices they considered offensive. Those included impersonating Indians, taking Indian names, combining elements of different cultures, assuming that the Lakota represented all Indians, and portraying Indians as being on the verge of extinction and thus in need of White people to preserve their traditions—all features of Flying Cloud.[57] Perhaps nothing so clearly demonstrates the indifference of most eastern progressives to Native American issues as the continuation of those practices at the camps for many years.[58]

DISMANTLING THE INDIAN PROGRAM

But there were always rumblings of dissent. According to Rick Hausman, controversy about the Indian programming had "plagued" Flying Cloud since its establishment.[59] In the 1990s, the staff instituted the first of two major reforms. "Opening the Door to the East" responded to the criticism that Lakota traditions had no place at a Vermont camp. Seeking to orient the Indian program toward the culture of northeastern forest tribes, the camp hired Dana Pictou, a Micmac Native American originally from Nova Scotia but now living in Vermont. One camper later described the thrill of watching him demonstrate basket weaving: "I remember starting the day with a whole ash log and ending with a basket—incredible process."[60] According to Nate Hausman, Pictou's responsibilities soon grew to include leading the camp's opening and closing ceremonies and holding sweat lodges.

The second and more extensive reform began during Mathon's directorship. Mathon traces his own conversion to a talk he heard at a meeting of all F&W directors in the middle of the summer of 2000.[61] The speaker was a young woman of Hmong descent who had been an IB camper and counselor and was now working for Crossroads Ministry (later Crossroads Antiracism Organizing and Training). "In a moment of deep graciousness, but also calling to action," Mathon said, "she shared her story which was that as a young girl and as a young woman, both as camper and counselor, she had loved her experiences at IB, cherished them, grew with them. The experiences themselves were part of the reason she had moved on professionally to become an anti-racism trainer." As a young woman of color, however, she also had experienced "both individual and organizational racism," and she "challenged us to really dig into the roots of the social justice underpinnings of F&W and to say, 'If you are going to be true to your word, what your vision is, you need to do some work.'" The directors decided that they all should attend a two-and-a-half-day antiracism training in Chicago held by the Crossroads Ministry the following February.

Mathon later wrote that as the weekend progressed, he began to ask questions such as the following: "What are we doing at Flying Cloud? Are we being respectful of the traditions of people who have had everything stripped from them—including their traditions and cultures? Are we simply having fun in the woods? . . . Are we doing enough to raise awareness with our predominantly white campers and staff of the historical and present day struggles of American Indians? Are we allies to American Indians in their struggle to maintain their cultures and identities today—locally, nationally?"[62] Realizing that he did not have the answers, Mathon took various steps. He began reading about Native American activism and cultural appropriation. He canvassed the previous Flying Cloud directors to ask how they thought he should proceed. "That told me," he said, "that I wasn't alone and I had not a mandate, but some sense of common purpose around not knowing what the changes could or should be, but at least asking very hard deep questions." He had a conversation with Dana Pictou and his partner Lorraine, who also had worked at the camp, where he "shared what I had experienced and learned and read about. My memory is that both of them were just nodding their heads. My interpretation is, 'Well, I'm glad you finally have gotten some light. I'm glad you've finally gotten to see something that we've known all along.' He was clear in those conversations that he saw the beauty of what Flying Cloud was and saw the impact on young men and boys, but he had lived with discomfort every time he came." Dana Pictou agreed to continue leading opening and closing ceremonies but refused to conduct more sweat lodges.

Nate Hausman, Flying Cloud's assistant director, recalled that Pictou's announcement prompted a further "soul searching." Nate's letter that spring opened with the salutation "Howdy Campers." "When I first heard of Dana's decision," he wrote,

> I had some serious reservations about camp starting this summer. Dana has been one of my most influential spiritual teachers and has been at Flying Cloud as long as I have. As a result, it is hard for me to imagine FC without him. However, Dana's decision was not about him leaving Flying Cloud. It was about him opting not to be a sweat lodge leader for a non-Native summer camp claiming to have a stake in his culture's spirituality. We can continue to learn from Dana's spirituality so long as we recognize that it is his people's spirituality. Flying Cloud can provide the kind of spiritual growth it does for boys, but we can no longer afford to do it by stealing native culture, heritage, and rituals.[63]

When the summer 2001 session opened, Mathon began the process of shedding Indian practices and symbols. He explained why he ended the tradition of wearing loincloths: "On the one hand, breechcloths represented a simple, down-to-earth, practical piece of clothing that also provided a visual, and sometimes ceremonial, connection between Fc'ers. On the other hand, it was difficult for many, including myself to look at using breechcloths and not simply see a bunch of boys playing Indian."[64] There was less ambivalence about replacing tipis. "While tipis themselves are clearly romantic dwellings," Jane Wohl wrote, "they are not, as anyone of us who has lived in them knows, ideal for Vermont summers. The high plains get very little rain in the summers, as opposed to soggy Vermont, and tipis are often damp and sometimes flooded."[65] By 2001, even the poles were rotting.[66] Mathon also realized that the "flag song, which Allen Flying By had introduced back in '89 had to go." As a result, Mathon told us, "We actually spent some of that summer kind of creating new songs and thinking through how to do that." In addition, he insisted that the campers learn history. "We had big, giant, not whiteboards, but like foam core boards, that we wrote big histories on, and then did presentations . . . about the genocide and cultural appropriation." He especially wanted "to make sure people knew that Indian people still existed." The one clear message he had heard from Native American activists was "We are still here, we are still strong, we are still experiencing pain, we are still experiencing joy."

Those changes generated mixed emotions. Nate Hausman had followed Mathon as director and continued the process of reform. Although Nate's father, Rick, told us that he and his son "weren't exactly at loggerheads," he acknowledged that he "was trying to find my way through this change, but it was very hard for me to accept, just the drumming and the music associated with the camp was so powerful, and losing all of that was difficult." Later in the interview, he added that the change "also was difficult because I struggled with, what did I do wrong? Where was my conception incorrect and insensitive and just erroneous?" Wakio's grandson, Tsiorasa Barreiro, worried that his grandfather's legacy might be diminished. "As a former camper," he told F&W executive director Rebecca Geary in 2020, "I didn't want my grandfather's investment and love of F&W to be . . . put in the corner. It seemed that this reaction was an overcorrection, perhaps, and could lead to my grandfather's connection with F & W being reduced."[67] Like many people who remembered participating in Indian rituals in other youth organizations (the Boy Scouts, YMCA-Indian Guides, and Camp Fire Girls), several Flying Cloud alumni argued that the discarded practices had had deep personal significance to them. Jane Wohl commented that she, too, was "disappointed to see the whole naming ceremony banned." The "process of coming up with the names" had been an important one for the staff. "We sat around and thought about those names and thought hard about what those kids' strengths were."[68] Just before we spoke, she had received a phone call from a man who had been a thirteen-year-old camper in 1969. Although his life had changed greatly since then, the name "He Looks Both Ways" still fit.

By the early 2000s, however, supporters of Indian programming were clearly on the defensive. The staff had firmly resolved to expunge Indian iconography while retaining what they considered the Flying Cloud's core values. In 2002, Sunshine Mathon listed those as "simplicity and isolation, respect and community, a common gender, honoring the land, and honoring the spirit."[69]

CONCLUSION

Although Farm & Wilderness followed a long line of summer camps offering Indian lore, the establishment of Flying Cloud, based almost entirely on Indian practices and symbols, represented an unusual enterprise. Soon after the camp opened, Native American activists pointed out that the appropriation of Indian rituals by non-Indians was offensive and harmful. Just as Farm & Wilderness as a whole attempted to move beyond the ideology of color blindness in relating to Black campers, so Flying Cloud eventually heeded the arguments of Native American critics. But the elimination of Indian themes at Flying Cloud occurred decades later than F&W's attempts to respond to Black demands. In the 1970s, when Farm & Wilderness staff were trying to fight racism by making the program more relevant to Black campers, Flying Cloud leaders ignored the Native American protests that arose in the same decade. One reason may be that even progressive easterners viewed race exclusively in terms of Black/White relations. Another may be that Flying Cloud had too few Native American campers or counselors who could press for change. Moreover, because the counselors were paid to bring Indian lore to the camps, they stood to lose a significant share of their livelihood if they voiced their objections. Dana Pictou's decision to stop leading sweat lodge ceremonies thus represented a critical turning point.

In 2019, Rebecca Geary, the Farm & Wilderness executive director, toured the Akwesasne reservation in northern New York with Wakio's grandson Tsiorasa Barreiro, executive director of the tribe. The two then established a formal partnership between their organizations.[70] Even before that event, Wakio's family retained a presence at F&W. Many of his children and grandchildren were campers. One of those was his youngest daughter Katsi Cook, who is nationally and internationally recognized for her work at the intersection of reproductive rights and environmental justice. She was an Indian Brook camper in 1964, a Dark Meadow counselor in 1971, and a member of the F&W board of trustees between 2019 and 2022. Like many members of her father's generation, she immersed herself in Indigenous culture. Her primary goal, however, was to empower her community to address critical contemporary concerns. She told an interviewer in 2005 that she wanted "to learn what is it in our knowledge base that can have an impact on our life, everyday life, and not just something you hang in a museum or talk about in a nice class" (or, we might add, teach to White campers).[71] Moreover, although Flying Cloud has always been for boys alone, Katsi emphasized that traditional Mohawk society was matrilineal and matrilocal. "It's our duty as mothers," she stated, "to maintain in our children the knowledge systems that come from our ancestors."[72] A midwife as well as a political activist, she sought to integrate Indigenous knowledge with biomedical protocols in her practice. One of her many achievements was leading a groundbreaking study of the impact of Polychlorinated biphenyls (PCBs) and heavy-metal pollutants on the breast milk of Native American women living near the St. Lawrence River. As she then declared, "Women are the first environment."[73]

CONCLUSION

Walking through the camps while we were gathering material for this book, it was easy to forget that more than half a century had elapsed since we were campers and counselors. True, new buildings had appeared, and many old ones had been refurbished. But we saw the same steep dirt paths that had seemed so treacherous at night, the same open cabins hidden in the woods, and the same stunning views of the lake from various points. What remained invisible were the myriad ways the camps had undergone transformation as successive generations had struggled to align the Webbs' values with changing political understandings and shifts in culture and society.

Some of the Webbs' ideals remained intact: simplicity, challenging work, spirituality, cooperation, and social justice. Others, however, had to be reevaluated and reconfigured. We saw this first when we examined the notion of color blindness. Like the directors of subsidized camps who were the first to enroll Black children in previously all-White camps, the Webbs acted as if racial justice could best be served by encouraging campers to ignore the issue of race. Our interviewees who had attended Farm & Wilderness in the 1950s and early 1960s were acutely aware of racial differences. Almost none, however, remember discussing race. By the late 1960s and early 1970s, campers and counselors were forced to confront the topic directly both because Black and White campers often came from decidedly different backgrounds and because the broader landscape of race relations had changed dramatically. African American campers at Indian Brook demanded their own space and organized a hair salon for African American girls alone. The White staff suddenly realized that the old ways of dealing with race no longer were appropriate.

The Indian lore program had to be completely dismantled. Convinced that what was considered Native American culture had a great deal to teach White boys, Ken Webb invited a young Mohawk man to establish an Indian Village soon after Timberlake opened. In successive years, he expanded the Indian lore program. And then in 1965, Ken established Flying Cloud, an entire camp based as closely as possible on what were thought to be Native American traditions.

Long after Farm & Wilderness began to reconsider how to address Black/White relationships, the camp leadership ignored the growing chorus of activists who insisted that Whites stop "playing Indian." At the turn of the twenty-first century, however, the directors slowly removed the trappings of Native American culture from Flying Cloud.

The description of Flying Cloud on the F&W website today makes no mention of Native Americans. Instead, it reads, "Flying Cloud Camp celebrates everyone, as they are, exploring the wonder of living in nature together. . . . Surrounded by hundreds of acres of wilderness, campers tap into their curiosity and imagination with unscripted days spent coaxing an ember into fire, carving their own eating utensils and witnessing the beauty of the Vermont sky at night. Camp life unfolds simply with games and adventures from sunrise to starlight, in a gentle, unrushed community." The few remaining shelters that formerly were called tipis now are known as "canvases."

Despite opposition from loyal alumni, F&W finally decided to change the name "Indian Brook." Announcing in 2021 that the camp would be called "IB" until a new name could be found, the board noted that "several things have occurred, not the least of which is that the world has gained a deeper understanding of systemic inequality and discrimination, and the role names play in how we see each other."[1] The new name, Firefly Song, was revealed at a banquet at the end of the 2022 summer. In a letter to the Indian Brook community,

FIGURE 14. Flying Cloud campers erecting a canvas. Photograph courtesy of Nate Hausman.

Frances McLaughlin, F&W executive director, wrote that the new name "will gently light the way of campers and enable them to see the light in themselves and each other at all times."[2] In addition, she added that it "harkens back to the 'Lightning Bug,' still a prized camp memento, . . . connects 'light' to F&W's value of 'peace,' . . . lifts up song, which is such an integral part of camp here [and will] make campers and alumni remember summer nights and magical moments."

New understandings of gender as well as race and ethnicity required other changes. Susan Webb had an expansive view of women's capabilities. In the post–World War II era, when women's roles were severely restricted, she wanted girls to shed constrictive clothes, engage in strenuous work projects, and embark on rigorous hikes and canoe trips. Her notion of gender, however, came under challenge by those who demanded a more explicit form of feminism at Indian Brook. Later, campers and staff at both Tamarack Farm and Indian Brook began to question the implicit assumption of heterosexuality and found ways to make lesbianism more visible.

The current F&W website confronts the issue of gender identity directly, declaring the camps to be "gender inclusive" places that "offer our youth the opportunity to choose a camp environment that best supports their gender identity." The "gender resources" page defines key terms: assigned sex, gender non-binary, cisgender and transgender. Parents are asked to consider "which camp is right for your child." Before any of the camps are described, parents fill in the blanks: "In summer 2023, my child will be [select age] and identifies as [select gender identity]." A nine-year-old who identifies as female, for example, is directed to the Barn Day Camp (mixed gender, ages 4–10) or Firefly Song (female & gender non-binary, ages 9–14). A thirteen-year-old who identifies as gender nonbinary is directed to Firefly Song, Timberlake (male & gender non-binary, ages 9–14), Red Spruce Grove (female & gender non-binary, ages 11–14), Flying Cloud (male & gender non-binary, ages 11–14), and Saltash Mountain (mixed gender, ages 11–14).

In the wake of the allegations of molestation at Timberlake, F&W sent a letter to all former campers at TL to gather information about other cases of abuse. Subsequently, F&W developed policies to prevent such abuse from happening again at any of the camps. A document dated April 12, 2022, states that staff are mandated reporters of child abuse or neglect and that staff training will include such issues as appropriate interactions with campers. The "rule of three policy" is aimed precisely at the type of situation that enabled sexual abuse to occur in the past: "When interacting with an individual camper, an individual staff member must be within sight or sound of other people. If the need arises for a camper to be in a remote location with a staff member, there must always be at least one additional person present. The third person can be another camper or staff member."

When we asked our interviewees what features of Farm & Wilderness could have facilitated sex abuse, most pointed first to the practice that had been called the "Fifth Freedom." Although Ken, far more than Susan, enshrined it as a prominent practice at Timberlake, it also (at least in the form of "skinny-dipping") had a cherished place at other F&W camps. Not only might it have enabled molestation, but nudism also was the aspect of the camps that engendered the most ridicule from the local community. Moreover, it hindered F&W's attempts to attract campers from different racial and ethnic groups. Although many campers and counselors continued to argue that the Fifth Freedom was a vital part of the camps, the board banned the practice in 2007.

Those campers who came on scholarship in the first several decades of F&W might have been aware their families were getting assistance, but they did not necessarily feel that they were, in any way, "other." Subsequent directors argued that they could remain true to the social justice mission of Farm & Wilderness only if they enrolled campers from a broader range of households, including those whose parents were unskilled and poorly paid health care workers. For these campers, a summer at F&W often involved a significant transition to a new environment or to an association with very different peers, and sometimes both. The staff thus had to struggle to adhere to the original camp values while catering to a clientele that differed dramatically from the one the Webbs had selected.

Moreover, the camps never attended to social class as a matter of social dynamics as explicitly as they ultimately did to race. Many elite White institutions like prep schools and liberal arts colleges have struggled to find ways to make themselves welcoming to less privileged individuals. Usually, however, the difficulty comes from the unease the newcomers feel with the luxuries the institutions have to offer and the casual assumptions about the opportunities wealth provides. At Farm & Wilderness, the difficulty may have been something else: many middle-class campers enjoyed the challenge of doing without electricity and running water. (As we have seen, Ken frequently extolled the ruggedness of the camps as a way to toughen up children from affluent suburbs.) But those already living in less comfortable surroundings may have experienced F&W's privations very differently. And those whose families had recently achieved middle-class status might have considered life at F&W to be moving them in the wrong direction.

In addition to aligning older policies with newer conceptions of gender, sexuality, ethnicity, and race, F&W has sought to respond to other demands of contemporary life. Most of our peers came to camp for the full eight weeks; considerably fewer campers do so now. To encourage parents to send their children to camp for the entire summer (which is now six weeks), F&W offers a discount for those who sign up for two three-week sessions, whether at the same camp or divided between two different ones. Younger children (those coming for their first time to either Firefly Song or Timberlake at ages nine and ten) can come for a two-week period at the beginning of each of the three-week sessions. Children ages four to ten attend the Barn Day Camp Monday through Friday, for one- or two-week periods.

At the same time as the declining birth rate has diminished the size of the pool of potential campers, F&W competes with a larger number, and broader range, of camps.[3] The approximately seven thousand overnight summer camps in existence today are divided among a number of different categories, including "traditional camps"—offering such activities as ropes course, canoeing, swimming, arts and crafts, and campfire—academic and technology camps, travel and expedition camps, special needs camps, arts and performance camps, faith-based camps, military camps and police academies, Scouts camps, sports camps, camps for foster kids, and camps for teens.[4]

The COVID-19 pandemic forced F&W to close in the summer of 2020. When the camps reopened the following year, they faced new challenges. The additional health regulations that had been imposed were costly and cumbersome, and qualified counselors were in short supply. COVID-19 fears forced the executive director to cancel the annual fair midway through the 2022 session to protect campers and staff.

·

A major theme in the interviews we conducted was the profound impact Farm & Wilderness had had on many lives. Several people said their closest friendships were still the ones they had forged at camp. A few had met their life partners there. Tony Parkes commented that he was only one of the many callers and musicians whose interest in folk music and square dancing began at F&W. Joan Cannady Countryman recalled her experience at IB when she told the girls at the school she directed that they could do anything. As president of UNITE HERE, John Wilhelm drew on the political analyses he developed through his contact with F&W alumni. Skills honed in campcraft enabled Barry Wohl to find relief on weekend hiking trips from the stresses of his job as a pediatrician. Susan Fletcher credits F&W with enabling her to turn to nature for solace when her daughter was seriously ill. Others noted that silent morning meetings had made it easier for them to develop spiritual practices incorporating meditation. Although those who had survived abuse at F&W also mentioned friendships, music, politics, campcraft, and spirituality to explain why even they returned year after year, their overall assessment of the influence of F&W was more nuanced.

Over time, former campers and staff have had to confront challenges to the model of social justice F&W provided in its first several decades. Newer conceptions of gender, sexuality, class, ethnicity, and race have led to questions about earlier practices and assumptions. If experiences at F&W did not always provide the basis for a clear path forward, they might well have encouraged openness to the possibility of alternative ways of living.

ACKNOWLEDGMENTS

We are grateful to the people we interviewed (or who sent us comments) who are named in the manuscript: John Bancroft, Jean Coulter Brown, Len Cadwallader, Mary Ann Cadwallader, Joan Countryman, Steve Curwood, Peg Espinola, Janine Fay, David Finkelhor, Susan Fletcher, Ann Scattergood Fogg, Rick Hausman, Bob Hausman, Nate Hausman, Jon Jacques, Jimmy Klein, Tom Klein, Sunshine Mathon, Anne McElhinney, Carol Rapaport Monteleoni, Bill Nelson, Berl Nussbaum, Liz Ohle, Judy Polumbaum, Neil Rolnick, Kyle Rolnick, Helen Seitz, Paul Stone, Martyne Stout, Nick Thorkelson, John Wilhelm, Barry Wohl, and Jane Wohl.

We appreciate the many other people who gave us useful information but are not named in the manuscript: members of the TF'60 listserv, Sarah Ashe, Sarah Gates, Janet Green, Elizabeth Hersh, Ruth Hunter, Ellie Scattergood Lash, David Nussbaum, Miki Polumbaum, Jim Schine, Frances Stone, Topher Waring, Peggy Brown White, several informants who asked not to be quoted, and two who wished to remain anonymous.

We thank Robert Schine for sharing memories of Camp Darrow; Elizabeth Hersh, John Wilhelm, and Connie Brown for reading the manuscript before publication; Paul Stone, Frances Stone, John Wilhelm, Berl Nussbaum, Nate Hausman, Peg Espinola, Anne McElhinney, and Peggy Brown White for searching for pictures; Lori Terrill, librarian at the Leland D. Case Library, Black Hills State University, Spearfish, South Dakota, for xeroxing a copy of *The Indian Counselor Handbook* for us; William Boardman for permission to use a picture of Ken and Susan Webb; Ann Shalleck for talking through legal issues; and Peter Jaszi for significant legal help.

Emily thanks her history writing group—Carla Bittel, Charlotte Borst, Janet Brodie, Sharla Fett, Janet Golden, and Alice Wexler—for their comments and support.

NOTES

NOTES TO INTRODUCTION

1. Emily K. Abel and Margaret K. Nelson, *Limited Choices: Mable Jones, a Black Children's Nurse in a Northern White Household* (Charlottesville: University of Virginia Press, 2021).

2. See, for example, Marta Gutman and Ning de Coninck-Smith, eds., *Designing Modern Childhoods: History, Space, and the Material Culture of Children* (New Brunswick, N.J.: Rutgers University Press, 2008).

3. The phrase comes from Steven Mintz, *Huck's Raft: A History of American Childhood* (Cambridge, Mass.: Belknap Press of Harvard University Press, 2004), 275–276.

4. A woman we knew from our days at F&W sent us a copy of a letter her son had written from Timberlake, one of the F&W camps: "Dear Mom and Dad, I hate to start out this letter like this but I'm not having a very good time at camp."

5. See, for example, Christopher A. Thurber et al., "Youth Development Outcomes of the Camp Experience: Evidence for Multidimensional Growth," *Journal of Youth and Adolescence* 36, no. 3 (March 22, 2007): 241–254, https://doi.org/10.1007/s10964-006-9142-6; Karla A. Henderson, M. Deborah Bialeschki, and Penny A. James, "Overview of Camp Research," *Child and Adolescent Psychiatric Clinics of North America* 16, no. 4 (October 2007): 755–767, https://doi.org/10.1016/j.chc.2007.05.010; Karla A. Henderson et al., "Summer Camp Experiences: Parental Perceptions of Youth Development Outcomes," *Journal of Family Issues* 28, no. 8 (August 2007): 987–1007, https://doi.org/10.1177/0192513X07301428; Christine A. Readdick, "Summer Camp and Self-Esteem," *Perceptual and Motor Skills* 101, no. 5 (2005): 121, https://doi.org/10.2466/PMS.101.5.121-130; Barry A. Garst, Laurie P. Browne, and M. Deborah Bialeschki, "Youth Development and the Camp Experience," *New Directions for Youth Development* 2011, no. 130 (June 2011): 73–87, https://doi.org/10.1002/yd.398; and M. Deborah Bialeschki, Karla A. Henderson, and Penny A. James, "Camp Experiences and Developmental Outcomes for Youth," *Child and Adolescent Psychiatric Clinics of North America* 16, no. 4 (October 2007): 769–788, https://doi.org/10.1016/j.chc.2007.05.011.

6. Erving Goffman, *Asylums: Essays on the Social Situation of Mental Patients and Other Inmates*, 1st ed. (Garden City, N.Y.: Anchor, 1961), 22.

7. Randal K. Tillery, "Touring Arcadia: Elements of Discursive Simulation and Cultural Struggle at a Children's Summer Camp," *Cultural Anthropology* 7, no. 3 (1992): 381.

8. Leslie Paris, *Children's Nature: The Rise of the American Summer Camp*, 1st ed. (New York: New York University Press, 2010); Sharon Wall, *The Nurture of Nature: Childhood, Antimodernism, and Ontario Summer Camps, 1920–55* (Vancouver: University of British Columbia Press, 2009); Abigail A. Van Slyck, *A Manufactured Wilderness: Summer Camps and the Shaping of American Youth, 1890–1960*, 1st ed. (Minneapolis: University Of Minnesota Press, 2006).

9. Mintz, *Huck's Raft*.

10. Letter to Emily Abel, February 26, 2023.

11. Mindy Thompson Fullilove, *The House of Joshua: Meditations on Family and Place* (Lincoln: University of Nebraska Press, 1999), 127.

12. Susan Webb and Kenneth Webb, *Beyond Our Wildest Dreams: The Story of the Farm and Wilderness Camps, 1939–1989,* ed. and designed by Jane Curtis, Will Curtis, and Frank Lieberman for the Farm and Wilderness Foundation (Springfield, Vt.: Springfield Printing Corporation, 1989), hereafter *BOWD1989.*

13. Cookson Communications, "Summer Camp Ad Campaign," Farm & Wilderness, accessed September 9, 2022, https://cooksoncommunications.com/work/farm-and-wilderness/.

14. Len Cadwallader and Mary Ann Cadwallader, Zoom interview with authors, January 27, 2022.

15. Admittedly, this is a select group of interviewees and does not include either campers or staff whose affiliation was short-lived. This is by design: we wanted to speak with individuals who could reflect on the impact F&W had on their lives.

16. Webb and Webb, *BOWD1989.*

17. Susan Webb and Kenneth Webb, *Beyond Our Wildest Dreams: The Story of the Farm and Wilderness Camps, 1939–2021,* 2nd ed., revised and updated by Kristi Webb (Springfield, Vt.: Springfield Printing, 2021).

18. Frances McLaughlin, the executive director, wrote that the executive committee "hopes that you would be open to sharing a pre-publication copy of the book or other publications you author which focus on Farm & Wilderness." She continued, "*This would not, of course, be for purposes of approval or editing, as this is your project*" (emphasis added).

19. We described our research this way:

> We propose to write a social history of F&W camps from 1939 to the latter part of the 20th century. By that we mean we will look at the camps within the context of the times and trace the ways they changed in response to shifts in culture and society.
>
> Specific topics we will explore include spirituality, race, class, gender, and sexuality. We will also ask how the camps informed campers' engagement as political actors. We will draw on our own recollections, Ken and Susan Webbs' writings, interviews with campers, staff, board members, and directors during the relevant years, and whatever printed materials (including the *Interim, Lightning Bug, Thunderbird,* and directors' reports) are available in the camp archives.
>
> We are sisters who went to camp together; we have had long careers teaching and writing in the fields of sociology (Peggy) and history (Emily).

20. Webb and Webb, *BOWD1989.* In 1940, the cost was $250 ($4,875 in today's terms), or one-fifth of the median family income of $1,226 (1940 Census, table 1, "Families by Family Wage or Salary Income," 7).

21. Zoom Interview with authors, September 12, 2021.

NOTES TO CHAPTER 1

1. Massachusetts, U.S., Marriage Records, 1840–1915, Ancestry.com, accessed September 2, 2021.

2. Records of the Bureau of the Census, Record Group 29, *Tenth Census of the United States* (Washington, D.C.: National Archives, 1880), NARA microfilm publication T9, 1,454 rolls.

3. 1860 Census, Bridgeport, Fairfield, Connecticut (p. 251); 1870 Census, Birmingham, New Haven, Connecticut (roll M593_111, p. 117A); 1880 Census, Waterbury, New Haven, Connecticut (roll 103, p. 66A, Enumeration District 0361860); 1880 Census, Bridgeport, Fairfield, Connecticut (p. 251); 1870 Census, Birmingham, New Haven, Connecticut (roll M593_111,

p. 117A); 1880 Census, Waterbury, New Haven, Connecticut (roll 103, p. 66A, Enumeration District 036).

4. Susan H. Webb, *The Susan Howard Webb Story* (Barre, Vt.: Vermont Schoolhouse Press, 1998).

5. 1940 Census, Agawam, Hampden, Massachusetts (roll m-t0627-01593, p. 11B, Enumeration District 7-1).

6. Webb, *Susan Howard Webb Story.*

7. Webb.

8. Howard Family Tree, Ancestry.com, accessed September 3, 2021.

9. Webb, *Susan Howard Webb Story.*

10. Webb, 11.

11. For this history, see William Boardman, *WCS—Woodstock Country School: A History of Institutional Denial* (Toronto, Canada: Yorkland, 2016).

12. "Robert H. Webb, 1934–2018," Farm & Wilderness, accessed August 29, 2018, https://www.farmandwilderness.org/news-and-announcements/2018/08/29/robert-h-webb-1934-2018.

13. Kenneth B. Webb and Susan H. Webb, *Summer Magic: What Children Gain from Camp* (New York: Association Press, 1953); Kenneth Webb and Susan Webb, *The Boy Who Could Sleep When the Wind Blew* (Canaan, N.H.: Phoenix, 1963).

14. Kenneth Webb, *As Sparks Fly Upward: The Rationale of the Farm and Wilderness Camps* (Canaan, N.H.: Phoenix, 1973); Kenneth B. Webb, *From Plymouth Notch to President: The Farm Boyhood of Calvin Coolidge* (Taftsville, Vt.: Countryman, 1978).

15. Susan Webb and Kenneth Webb, *Beyond Our Wildest Dreams: The Story of the Farm and Wilderness Camps, 1939–1989* (Springfield, Vt.: Springfield Printing, 1989), hereafter *BOWD1989.*

16. Webb and Webb, 7.

17. Susan Webb and Kenneth Webb, *Beyond Our Wildest Dreams: The Story of the Farm and Wilderness Camps, 1939–2021*, 2nd ed., revised and updated by Kristi Webb (1989; repr., Springfield, Vt.: Springfield Printing, 2021).

18. Webb and Webb, *BOWD1989,* 10.

19. Webb and Webb, 10.

20. See especially Donna McDaniel and Vanessa Julye, *Fit for Freedom, Not for Friendship: Quakers, African Americans, and the Myth of Racial Justice* (Philadelphia: Quaker, 2009).

21. "American Friends Service Committee," *Densho Encyclopedia,* last modified March 3, 2015, https://encyclopedia.densho.org/American_Friends_Service_Committee/; "Friends Remembered: Quaker Journal Looks at Japanese American Internment," *AsianWeek,* March 5, 1993.

22. For the therapeutic cast of postwar camps in general, see Michael B. Smith, "'The Ego Ideal of the Good Camper' and the Nature of Summer Camp," *Environmental History* 11, no. 1 (January 2006): 85.

23. Ellen Herman, *The Romance of American Psychology: Political Culture in the Age of Experts* (Berkeley: University of California Press, 1995), 3.

24. Webb and Webb, *Summer Magic,* 41.

25. Kenneth B. Webb, "Sometimes It's Needed," *Christian Science Monitor,* May 17, 1958.

26. Kenneth B. Webb, "Children 'Find Themselves,'" *Christian Science Monitor,* December 5, 1959.

27. Webb and Webb, *Summer Magic,* 27.

28. Webb and Webb, *BOWD1989,* 28.

29. Leslie Paris, *Children's Nature: The Rise of the American Summer Camp* (New York: New York University Press, 2008), 226–256.

30. See Lawrence Cremin, *The Transformation of the School: Progressivism in American Education, 1876–1957* (New York: Vintage, 1964); Peter Gibbon, "John Dewey: Portrait of a Progressive Thinker," *Education Digest* 85, no. 3 (Jan/Feb 2020): 56–64; and Diane Ravitch, *The Troubled Crusade: American Education, 1945–1980* (New York: Basic Books, 1985).

31. Kenneth B. Webb, "Many a Camp Democratically Run, with Campers Taking Part," *Christian Science Monitor*, February 3, 1951.

32. Webb and Webb, *Summer Magic*, 13.

33. Kenneth B. Webb, "Challenges of Rustic Camping," *Christian Science Monitor*, May 8, 1965.

34. William Cronon, "The Trouble with Wilderness: Or, Getting Back to the Wrong Nature," *Environmental History* 1, no. 1 (January 1996): 7–28.

35. Quoted in Cronon, 14.

36. Webb and Webb, *Summer Magic*, 78.

37. Webb, *As Sparks Fly Upward*, 61.

38. Webb, 62.

39. Webb and Webb, *BOWD 1989*, 50–54.

40. Anne M. Hamilton, "Under the Shadow of Mount Saltash," Wilderness Community, 2008, https://wildernesscommunity.org/wp-content/uploads/2020/08/under-the-shadow-of-mount-saltash.pdf.

41. "Who We Are," Ninevah Foundation, accessed November 12, 2022, https://www.ninevahfoundation.org/who-we-are. In 1995, the private corporation became the nonprofit Ninevah Foundation.

42. Dona Brown, *Back to the Land: The Enduring Dream of Self-Sufficiency in Modern America* (Madison: University of Wisconsin Press, 2011), 24.

43. Brown.

44. Brown, 148–149.

45. Helen Nearing and Scott Nearing, *The Good Life: Helen and Scott Nearing's Sixty Years of Self-Sufficient Living* (New York: Schocken, 1989), with a new preface by Helen Nearing; Rebecca Kneale Gould, *At Home in Nature: Modern Homesteading and Spiritual Practice in America* (Berkeley: University of California Press, 2005).

46. Webb and Webb, *BOWD 1989*, 44–45.

47. Smith, "'Ego Ideal of the Good Camper,'" 70–101.

48. "The Rise of Suburbs," U.S. History II (American Yawp), accessed October 3, 2021, https://courses.lumenlearning.com/ushistory2ay/chapter/the-rise-of-suburbs-2/.

49. Quoted in Lizabeth Cohen, "The Rise of American Consumerism," American Experience, accessed November 3, 2021, https://www.pbs.org/wgbh/americanexperience/features/tupperware-consumer/.

50. Webb, "Challenges of Rustic Camping."

51. See Brian Q. Cannon, review of *Back to the Land*, by Dona Brown, *American Historical Review* 117, no. 3 (June 2012): 857–858.

52. Gould, *At Home in Nature*, 9.

53. Webb and Webb, *Summer Magic*, 66–67.

54. Kenneth B. Webb, ed., *Light from a Thousand Campfires* (New York: American Camping Association, 1961).

55. *Thunderbird*, F&W Archives, 1970, V, 32, no. 3.

56. Webb, *As Sparks Fly Upward*, 9–10.

57. Brian Hoffman, *Naked: A Cultural History of American Nudism* (New York: New York University Press, 2015).

58. Kenneth B. Webb, "Line 12 B—Tax Surcharge," in "Letters to the Editor," *Friends Journal*, February 1, 1969.

59. Webb.

60. Webb and Webb, *Summer Magic*, 60.

61. Webb, *As Sparks Fly Upward*, 108.

62. Samuel B. Hand, Anthony Marro, and Stephen C. Terry, eds., *Philip Hoff: How Red Turned Blue in the Green Mountain State* (Lebanon, N.H.: Castleton State College / University Press of New England, 2011), 11.

63. *Rutland Daily Herald*, Letters to the Editor, November 5, 1959.

64. *Rutland Daily Herald*, "Letter to the Editor," November 11, 1959, 8.

65. "History," The King's Daughters, accessed May 11, 2021, https://www.kingsdaughters .org/about-us/history/.

66. *Rutland Daily Herald*, Letters to the Editor, December 4, 1961.

67. Martin B. Duberman, *In White America, a Documentary Play* (New York: Samuel French, 1964). "Famed documentary play traces the American quest for racial equality from the earliest days of the republic to the Little Rock crisis of 1957, with dialogue drawn from historical letters, speeches, journals, songs and other personal accounts including recordings of former slaves." Tyler Peterson, "50th Anniversary Production of *IN WHITE AMERICA* to Play New Federal Theatre, 10/15–11/15," BWW News Desk, September 18, 2015, https://www .broadwayworld.com/article/50th-Anniversary-Production-of-IN-WHITE-AMERICA-to -Play-New-Federal-Theatre-1015-1115-20150918.

68. *Rutland Daily Herald*, Letters to the Editor, May 17, 1967.

69. "Reformer Throws Editorial Support to Hubert Humphrey," *Rutland Daily Herald*, October 23, 1968, 13.

70. Webb, *Susan Howard Webb Story*.

71. Tonia Gray et al., "Defining Moments: An Examination of the Gender Divide in Women's Contribution to Outdoor Education," *Research in Outdoor Education* 15 (2017): 47–71, https://doi.org/10.1353/roe.2017.0003.

72. "Susan Webb Honored by Vermont State Legislature," Farm & Wilderness, June 19, 2012, https://www.farmandwilderness.org/news-and-announcements/2012/06/19/susan-webb -honored-by-vermont-state-legislature.

73. Len Cadwallader and Mary Ann Cadwallader, Zoom interview with authors, January 27, 2022.

74. Webb, *Susan Howard Webb Story*.

75. Jane Wohl, Zoom interview with authors, January 6, 2022.

76. Helen Seitz, Zoom interview with authors, January 21, 2022.

77. Zoom interview with authors, August 23, 2021.

78. Peg Espinola, Zoom interview with authors, August 20, 2021.

79. Ann Scattergood Fogg, Zoom interview with authors, September 9, 2021.

80. "Susan Says," *Lightning Bug*, F&W Archives, 1960.

NOTES TO CHAPTER 2

1. Ken Webb, "My Own Book of Timberlake," (unpublished manuscript, 1941), in papers provided by Rick Hausman.

2. "Ken Sez," *Thunderbird*, no. 5, 1957.

3. "Ken Sez," *Thunderbird*, no. 3, 1958.

4. "Ken Sez," *Thunderbird*, no. 5, 1958.

5. "Ken Says," *Thunderbird*, no. 8, 1960.

6. "Ken Says," *Thunderbird*, no. 1, 1962.

7. "Ken Says," *Thunderbird*, no. 4, 1963.

8. "Ken Says," *Thunderbird*, no. 6, 1973.

9. Zoom interview with authors, November 10, 2021.

10. Letter to Emily Abel, February 26, 2023.

11. Junorhane, "Am I Wrong?," Live Journal, January 19, 2007, https://junorhane.livejournal .com/83158.html.

12. Bob Hausman and Rick Hausman, Zoom interview with authors, July 28, 2021.

13. Jane Wohl, Zoom interview with authors, January 6, 2022.

14. Abigail A. Van Slyck, *A Manufactured Wilderness: Summer Camps and the Shaping of American Youth, 1890–1960*, 1st ed. (Minneapolis: University of Minnesota Press, 2006), 34–35.

15. Judy Polumbaum, Zoom interview with authors, August 8, 2021.

16. Cindy Amatniek, letter to "Indian Brook Friends," accessed September 29, 2021, https:// myemail.constantcontact.com/The-summer-of-1968-at-Indian-Brook--what-summer-do-you -remember-the-most---.html?soid=1102937022104&aid=Gc_Z8FeHe5k.

17. Janine Fay, Zoom interview with authors, January 12, 2022.

18. "Ken Sezs," *Thunderbird*, no. 1, 1956.

19. Cathy Wilkerson, *Flying Close to the Sun: My Life and Times as a Weatherman* (New York: Seven Stories, 2011), 36.

20. Peg Espinola, Zoom interview with authors, August 20, 2021.

21. Carol Rapaport Monteleoni, Zoom interview with authors, August 16, 2021.

22. Fay, Zoom interview with authors.

23. Helen Seitz, Zoom interview with authors, January 21, 2022.

24. Susan Webb and Kenneth Webb, *Beyond Our Wildest Dreams: The Story of the Farm and Wilderness Camps, 1939–1989*, ed. and designed by Jane Curtis, Will Curtis, and Frank Lieber- man (Springfield, Vt.: Springfield Printing Corporation, 1989), 60–61, hereafter *BOWD 1989*.

25. Mindy Thompson Fullilove, *The House of Joshua: Meditations on Family and Place* (Lin- coln, Neb.: University of Nebraska Press, 2002), 125.

26. Fullilove, 131.

27. David Finkelhor, Zoom interview with authors, January 13, 2022.

28. Barry Wohl, Zoom interview with authors, January 14, 2022.

29. Neil Rolnick, Zoom interview with authors, February 4, 2022.

30. Laurie Kahn, *Sleepaway: The Girls of Summer and Camps They Love*, 1st ed. (New York: Workman, 2003), 40–41.

31. Ricky Rogers, "News from Indian Lake," *Lightning Bug*, 1968.

32. P. L., "The Value of Work Projects," *SEWOCA*, 1952.

33. Dave Kuhn, "Preface," *SEWOCA*, 1968.

34. Susan Fletcher, Zoom interview with authors, December 10, 2021.

35. Ann Scattergood Fogg, Zoom Interview with authors, September 9, 2021.

36. Oxford Reference, s.v. "Gotrocks," accessed September 12, 2022, https://www.oxford reference.com/view/10.1093/acref/9780199916108.001.0001/acref-9780199916108-e-3442.

37. Wilkerson, *Flying Close*, 34.

38. Norm Williams, "What's It All About," *SEWOCA*, 1963.

NOTES TO CHAPTER 3

1. Susan Webb and Kenneth Webb, *Beyond Our Wildest Dreams: The Story of the Farm and Wilderness Camps, 1939–1989*, ed. and designed by Jane Curtis, Will Curtis, and Frank Lieberman (Springfield, Vt.: Springfield Printing Corporation, 1989), 64, hereafter *BOWD1989*.

2. Zoom interview with authors, October 8, 2021.

3. *Contra Pulse*, episode 23, "Tony Parkes," CDSS Podcasts, aired February 10, 2021, https://cdss.org/podcasts/podcast/episode-23-tony-parkes/.

4. "Neil Rolnick," NYU Steinhardt, accessed October 4, 2021, https://steinhardt.nyu.edu/people/neil-rolnick.

5. Thomas S. Curren, "'Broadside' of Boston, Folk Music and Coffeehouse News: An Introduction," Folk New England, 2015, https://folknewengland.org/archives/the-broadside-collection/about-the-broadside-of-boston/.

6. Robert Cantwell, *When We Were Good: The Folk Revival* (Cambridge, Mass.: Harvard University Press, 1996), 291.

7. John Wilhelm, Zoom interview with authors, September 18, 2021.

8. Cathy Wilkerson, *Flying Close to the Sun: My Life and Times as a Weatherman* (New York: Seven Stories, 2007), 34.

9. Ron Eyerman and Scott Barretta, "From the 30s to the 60s: The Folk Music Revival in the United States," *Theory and Society* 25, no. 4 (1996): 502.

10. Crystal Galyean, "'This Machine Kills Fascists': The Life and Music of Woody Guthrie," accessed November 3, 2021, https://ushistoryscene.com/article/woody-guthrie/.

11. Jon Pareles, "Pete Seeger, Champion of Folk Music and Social Change, Dies at 94," *New York Times*, January 28, 2014.

12. Tim Weiner, "Odetta, Voice of the Civil Rights Movement, Dies at 77," *New York Times*, December 3, 2008.

13. "Miriam Makeba, South African Singer," *Encyclopaedia Britannica*, June 3, 2021, https://www.britannica.com/biography/Miriam-Makeba.

14. Cindy Amatniek, letter to "Indian Brook Friends," accessed June 3, 2021, https://myemail.constantcontact.com/The-summer-of-1968-at-Indian-Brook--what-summer-do-you-remember-the-most---.html?soid=1102937022104&aid=Gc_Z8FeHe5k.

15. "Current Events," *Thunderbird*, August 25, 1976.

16. Berl Nussbaum, Zoom interview with authors, January 14, 2022.

17. Wilkerson, *Flying Close*, 50–51.

18. Carol Rapaport Monteleoni, Zoom interview with authors, August 16, 2021.

19. Wilkerson, *Flying Close*, 35.

20. Barry Wohl, Zoom interview with authors, September 8, 2021.

21. Jon Jacques, letter to Peggy Nelson, September 19, 2022.

22. Janine Fay, Zoom interview with authors, January 12, 2022.

23. Nick Thorkelson, Zoom interview with authors, September 6, 2021.

24. Zoom interview with authors, October 9, 2021.

25. Joan Cannady Countryman, Zoom interview with authors, September 17, 2021.

26. Neil Rolnick, Zoom interview with authors, February 4, 2022.

27. Kenneth B. Webb, "Camping for American Youth," F&W Archives, manuscript of Publications Committee, American Camp Association, 1961.

28. Steve Curwood, Zoom interview with authors, February 22, 2022.

29. "Susan Says," *Lightning Bug*, n.d.

30. Kenneth B. Webb, "Thoughtfully Run Camp Can Awaken a Child's Spiritual Awareness," *Christian Science Monitor*, May 28, 1949.

31. Monteleoni, Zoom interview with authors.

32. Amatniek, letter.

33. Judy Polumbaum, Zoom Interview with authors, August 8, 2021.

34. John Bancroft, Zoom interview with authors, September 16, 2021.

35. Ann Scattergood Fogg, Zoom interview with authors, September 9, 2021.

36. Wilkerson, *Flying Close*, 35.

37. Mindy Thompson Fullilove, *The House of Joshua: Meditations on Family and Place* (Lincoln: University of Nebraska Press, 1999), 130.

38. Susan Fletcher, Zoom interview with authors, December 10, 2021.

39. Fullilove, 129.

40. Wilkerson, *Flying Close*, 35.

41. Webb and Webb, *BOWD 1989*, 37.

42. Robert Wuthnow, *After Heaven—Spirituality in America since the 1950s* (Berkeley: University of California Press, 1998).

43. Elaine Tyler May, *Homeward Bound: American Families in the Cold War Era* (New York: Basic Books, 2008), 29.

44. Wuthnow, *After Heaven*.

45. Liz Ohle, Zoom interview with authors, August 3, 2021.

46. Liz Ohle, "Liz Ohle Faith Story March 24th," Cochran Street United Church, March 25, 2019, https://www.cochranestreetuc.com/sermons/2019/3/25/liz-ohle-faith-story-march-24th.

47. Peg Espinola, Zoom interview with authors, August 20, 2021.

48. Anne McElhinney, Zoom interview with authors, January 29, 2022.

49. Jennifer Blecher, *Camp Famous* (New York: Greenwillow, 2022).

50. Niki Harris and Doris Malin, *Someone Is Stealing My Summer* (independently published, 2022).

51. Joanne Levy, *The Sun Will Come Out* (Custer, Wash.: Orca Book, 2021).

52. Jane Wohl, Zoom interview with authors, January 6, 2022.

53. Helen Seitz, Zoom interview with authors, January 21, 2022.

54. Jean Coulter Brown, letter to Peggy Nelson, October 18, 2022.

55. Nate Hausman, Zoom interview with authors, December 2, 2021.

NOTES TO CHAPTER 4

1. "Indian Brook Brochure," 1941, in possession of authors.

2. Leslie Paris, *Children's Nature: The Rise of the American Summer Camp* (New York: New York University Press, 2010), 151.

3. Paris, 50.

4. Paris, 51.

5. "Service Projects," *Lightning Bug*, 1955.

6. "Joan Countryman: Oral History with Emma Lapsansky-Werner," *Quakers of Color International Archive (MS 1095)*, Special Collections and University Archives, University of Massachusetts Amherst Libraries, June 29, 2019, video, 43:05, https://www.chicagomanualofstyle.org/tools_citationguide/citation-guide-1.html#cg-book.

7. Jane Wohl, Zoom interview with authors, January 6, 2022.

8. Martyne Stout, Zoom interview with authors, September 11, 2021.

9. Steven Mintz, *Huck's Raft: A History of American Childhood* (Cambridge, Mass.: Harvard University Press, 2008), 286.

10. Rickie Solinger, *Wake up Little Susie: Single Pregnancy and Race Before Roe v. Wade* (New York: Routledge, 1992).

11. Phyllis Richman, "Answering Harvard's Question about My Personal Life, 52 Years Later," *Washington Post*, June 6, 2013.

12. Richman.

13. "Phyllis Richman Was Not Alone," *Washington Post*, June 11, 2013.

14. Sara Ruddick and Pamela Daniels, eds., *Working It Out: 23 Women Writers, Artists, Scientists, and Scholars Talk about Their Lives and Work* (New York: Pantheon, 1977).

15. Ruddick and Daniels, 81.

16. Evelyn Fox Keller, "The Anomaly of a Woman in Physics," in *Working It Out*, 77–91, quotation on p. 80.

17. Ann Scattergood Fogg, Zoom interview with authors, September 9, 2021.

18. Carol Rapaport Monteleoni, Zoom interview with authors, August 16, 2021.

19. Janine Fay, Zoom interview with authors, January 12, 2022.

20. Martyne Stout, Zoom interview with authors, September 11, 2021.

21. Susan Webb and Kenneth Webb, *Beyond Our Wildest Dreams: The Story of the Farm and Wilderness Camps, 1939–1989*, ed. and designed by Jane Curtis, Will Curtis, and Frank Lieberman (Springfield, Vt.: Springfield Printing Corporation, 1989), 66, hereafter *BOWD1989*.

22. Liz Ohle, Zoom interview with authors, August 3, 2021.

23. Kenneth B. Webb and Susan H. Webb, *Summer Magic: What Children Gain from Camp* (New York: Association Press, 1953), 34.

24. Webb and Webb, 37.

25. Emily Harnett, "Married to the Momism," *Lapham's Quarterly*, July 23, 2020.

26. Rebecca Jo Plant, *Mom: The Transformation of Motherhood in Modern America* (Chicago: University of Chicago Press, 2010), 19.

27. Webb and Webb, *Summer Magic*, 38.

28. Webb and Webb, 21.

29. Webb and Webb, 133, 138.

30. Mindy Thompson Fullilove, *The House of Joshua: Meditations on Family and Place* (Lincoln: University of Nebraska Press, 1999), 132.

31. Sarah Yahn, "The Evolution of Flying Cloud," *Seven Days*, August 19, 2009.

32. Elaine Tyler May, *Homeward Bound: American Families in the Cold War Era* (New York: Basic Books, 1988), 97.

33. Webb and Webb, *Summer Magic*, 72.

34. Kenneth B. Webb, *As Sparks Fly Upward: The Rationale of the Farm and Wilderness Camps* (Canaan, N.H.: Phoenix Publishing, 1973), 83.

35. Peg Espinola, Zoom interview with authors, August 20, 2021.

36. Zoom interview with authors, March 12, 2022.

37. Zoom interview with authors, December 10, 2021.

38. Liz Ohle, Zoom interview with authors, January 11, 2022.

39. Liz Ohle, "Putting Everyone in the Picture: Countering Homophobia in the Camp Setting," *Camping Magazine*, November/December 1990, 30–31.

40. *Camping Magazine*, "Letters to the Editor," January 1991, February 1991, March 1991, April 1991.

41. Michael Bronski, *Queer History of the United States* (Boston, Mass.: Beacon Press, 2011), 208.

42. Bronski, 219.

43. John D'Emilio and Estelle B Freedman, *Intimate Matters: A History of Sexuality in America* (Chicago: University of Chicago Press, 2013), 316.

44. Lillian Faderman, *The Gay Revolution: The Story of the Struggle* (New York: Simon & Schuster, n.d.), 233.

45. Fogg, Zoom interview with authors.

46. D'Emilio and Freedman, *Intimate Matters*, 354.

47. D'Emilio and Freedman, 355.

48. Anne McElhinney, Zoom interview with authors, January 29, 2022.

49. Len Cadwallader and Mary Ann Cadwallader, Zoom interview with authors, January 27, 2022.

50. Zoom interview with authors, January 5, 2022.

51. Zoom interview with authors, August 7, 2021.

NOTES TO CHAPTER 5

1 Tom Klein, telephone interview with authors, February 2, 2022; Jimmy Klein, telephone interview with authors, February 4, 2022.

2. Cited in a letter from John Bancroft to Ben Hirst and Steve Bushey, Vermont Department of Corrections, Len Cadwallader, Executive Director, Farm & Wilderness Camps, Kenneth Kruckemeyer, Clerk, Board of Trustees, F&W Camps Fellow Victims of Sexual Abuse by Jack Sloanaker, March 6, 1994 (John Bancroft, personal files).

3. "Camp Counselor Makes Plea Agreement," *Rutland Daily Herald*, May 21, 1994, 6.

4. "Former Counselor Faces More Allegations," *Rutland Daily Herald*, March 15, 1994, 6.

5. John Bancroft, Zoom interview with authors, September 16, 2021.

6. Len Cadwallader and Mary Ann Cadwallader, Zoom interview with authors, January 27, 2022.

7. "Camp Counselor Makes Plea Agreement," 7.

8. "Ex Counselor Gets Year in Jail for Molestation," *Rutland Daily Herald*, July 1, 1994, 5.

9. Telephone interview with John Bancroft, March 13, 2022.

10. "Ex Counselor Gets Year," 5.

11. "Ex Counselor Gets Year," 5.

12. "Ex Counselor Gets Year," 5.

13. See chapter 4, where we discuss how Indian Brook had responded to an occasion of a counselor "cuddling" with a camper.

14. Today, experts estimate that one in seven girls and one in twenty-five boys are sexually abused before they reach eighteen (Jane Long Weatherred, "Child Sexual Abuse and the Media: A Literature Review," *Journal of Child Sexual Abuse* 24, no. 1 [2015]: 18). According to a *Lancet* article, "Pain and tissue injury from child sexual abuse can completely heal in time, but psychological and medical consequences can persist through adulthood. Associated sexually transmitted diseases (such as HIV) and suicide attempts can be fatal" (Charles Felzen Johnson, "Child Sexual Abuse," *Lancet* 364. [July 31, 2004]: 462–470).

15. C. Henry Kempe et al., "The Battered-Child Syndrome," *Journal of the American Medical Association* 181, no. 1 (July 7, 1962): 17–24.

16. Katherine Beckett, "Culture and the Politics of Signification: The Case of Child Sexual Abuse," *Social Problems* 43, no. 1 (February 1996): 57–76.

17. Weatherred, "Child Sexual Abuse," 19.

18. Ross Cheit, *The Witch-Hunt Narrative: Politics, Psychology, and the Sexual Abuse of Children* (New York: Oxford University Press, 2014); Emily Bazelon, "Abuse Cases, and a Legacy of Skepticism," *New York Times*, June 9, 2014. Some sociologists use the term "moral panic" to explain what they view as the exaggerated response to the McMartin trial verdicts. See Philip

Jenkins, *Moral Panic: Changing Concepts of the Child Molester in Modern America* (New Haven, Conn.: Yale University Press, 1989).

19. Weatherred, "Child Sexual Abuse," 20.

20. Marci Hamilton, "History of U.S. Child Sex Abuse Statutes of Limitation Reform: 2002 to 2020," Child USA, February 26, 2021, p. 4, https://childusa.org/wp-content/uploads/2021/02/2021-02-26-2020-SOL-Report-2.16.21-v2-1.pdf.

21. Matt Keyser, "Timeline: A History of Priest Sex Abuse in the Catholic Church," KHOU 11, January 31, 2019, https://www.khou.com/article/news/nation-world/timeline-a-history-of-priest-child-sex-abuse-in-the-catholic-church/285-95a5c09f-cb56-40ee-be2a-9835cdff3e1c.

22. Eliana Dockterman, "These Men Say the Boy Scouts' Sex Abuse Problem Is Worse Than Anyone Knows," *Time*, June 1, 2019.

23. "The 'Perversion Files' Come to Light," *New York Times*, October 19, 2012.

24. Maria Chutchian, "U.S. Judge Signs off on $850 Million Boy Scouts Sex Abuse Settlement," Reuters, August 19, 2021, https://www.reuters.com/legal/transactional/boy-scouts-bankruptcy-judge-rule-850-million-sex-abuse-deal-2021-08-19/.

25. Bill Chappell, "Penn State Abuse Scandal: A Guide and Timeline," NPR, June 21, 2012, https://www.npr.org/2011/11/08/142111804/penn-state-abuse-scandal-a-guide-and-timeline.

26. Amos Kamil, "Prep-School Predators," *New York Times Magazine*, June 6, 2012. See Caitlin Flanagan, "The Dark Hallways of Horace Mann," *Atlantic*, January/February 2016.

27. Amos Kamil and Sean Elder, *Great Is the Truth: Secrecy, Scandal, and the Quest for Justice at the Horace Mann School* (New York: Farrar, Straus and Giroux, 2015).

28. Marc Fisher, "The Master: A Charismatic Teacher Enthralled His Students. Was He Abusing Them?," *New Yorker*, April 1, 2013.

29. Valerie Strauss, "An Extraordinary Story of Alleged Sex Abuse of Students at Elite Private School over Decades," *Washington Post*, May 27, 2015.

30. Mike Baker, "Sex-Abuse Claims against Boy Scouts Now Surpass 82,000," *Time*, November 15, 2020. See "Scout Leader Sentence 15 Years for Molesting," *Sarasota Herald Tribune*, June 13, 1982; Peter Zuckerman, "Scouts Honor," *Idaho Falls Post Register*, July 13, 2006; Dockterman, "Boy Scouts' Sex Abuse Problem"; Frank Donnelly, "Camping-Trip Nightmare: Former S. I. Boy Scout Alleges He Was Abused on Outings," Silive.com, August 10, 2021, https://www.silive.com/news/2021/08/camping-trips-nightmare-former-si-boy-scout-alleges-he-was-abused-on-outings.html; and Patricia Borns, "'Our Little Secret.' Eagle Scout Says Writing Graphic Book about Sex Abuse Helped Him Heal," *News-Press*, November 5, 2019, https://www.news-press.com/story/news/local/2019/11/05/sex-abuse-boy-scout-aaron-averhart/3985497002/.

31. "Hundreds of Sexual Abuse Cases Reported at Children's Camps across U.S.," *CBS Mornings*, December 10, 2018.

32. "Molestation and Abuse by Camp Counselors Is a National Epidemic," accessed June 2, 2021, https://crime-stoppers.org/wp-content/uploads/2019/10/Spreadsheet-of-Camp-Molestations-8-5-2019.pdf.

33. Leah Howell, "Are Your Kids Safe at Summer Camp?," Children's Advocacy Center, accessed June 2, 2021, https://cacjc.org/are-your-kids-safe-at-summer-camp/.

34. Rick Hausman and Bob Hausman, Zoom interview with authors, July 28, 2021.

35. Kurt Eichenwald, "On the Web, Pedophiles Extend Their Reach," *New York Times*, August 21, 2006.

36. Zoom interview with authors, February 6, 2022.

37. Zoom interview with authors, March 9, 2022.

38. Martyne Stout, Zoom interview with authors, September 11, 2021.

39. "Camp Counselor Makes Plea Agreement," *Rutland Daily Herald*, May 21, 1994, 6.

40. Zoom interview with authors, September 9, 2021.

41. David French and Nancy French, "They Aren't Who You Think They Are," *Dispatch*, March 28, 2021.

42. Kamil and Elder, *Great Is the Truth*, 41, 62.

43. Kamil and Elder, 82.

44. See Park Dietz, "Grooming and Seduction," *Journal of Interpersonal Violence* 33, no. 1 (2018): 28–36.

45. Baker, "Sex-Abuse Claims"; Kamil and Elder, *Great Is the Truth*, 35.

46. Dockterman, "Boy Scouts' Sex Abuse Problem."

47. Zoom interview with authors, February 8, 2022.

48. Kamil and Elder, *Great Is the Truth*, 88.

49. Rick Hausman and Bob Hausman, Zoom interview with authors, July 28, 2021.

50. Ann Scattergood Fogg, Zoom interview with authors, September 9, 2021.

51. Zoom interview with authors, January 5, 2022.

52. Nicholas Scurich and Park Dietz, "Psychological Barriers to the Detection of Child Sexual Abuse," SSRN, February 16, 2021, https://papers.ssrn.com/sol3/papers.cfm?abstract_id= 3786874.

53. Letter from John Bancroft to Ben Hirst and Steve Bushey (John Bancroft, personal files).

54. Hamilton, "U.S. Child Sex Abuse Statutes," 5.

55. Kamil, "Prep-School Predators."

56. Zoom interview with authors, January 14, 2022.

57. Telephone interview with Margaret Nelson, August 1, 2021.

58. Hamilton, "U.S. Child Sex Abuse Statutes"; Elizabeth A. Harris, "Sex Abuse Victims' Obstacle to Justice: The Clock," *New York Times*, December 5, 2017.

59. David Finkelhor, Zoom interview with authors, January 13, 2022.

60. French and French, "Who You Think They Are"; "Boy Scouts of America Sexual Abuse: Over 100 Years of Hidden Abuse," accessed June 4, 2021, https://abusedinscouting.com/history-of-abuse/.

61. Zoom interview with authors, March 15, 2022.

62. Kenneth B. Webb, "What Might the School Learn from Experience of the Camp?," *Christian Science Monitor*, June 19, 1948.

63. Bob Hausman and Rick Hausman, Zoom interview with authors, August 28, 2021.

64. Matt Hamilton et al., "A Betrayal of Trust: Report on Alleged Sexual Misconduct Reveals Reality behind Board School's Stated Values," *Los Angeles Times*, June 23, 2021.

65. Zoom interview with authors, August 7, 2021.

66. Neil Rolnick, Zoom interview with authors, February 2, 2022.

67. Letter from John Bancroft, 1994.

68. "Former Pope Benedict Failed to Act over Abuse, New Report Finds," *BBC News*, January 20, 2022.

69. Letter from John Bancroft, 1994.

70. Ron Roberts, Tom O'Connor, July Dunn, and Jean Golding, "The Effects of Child Sexual Abuse in Later Family Life; Mental Health, Parenting, and Adjustment of Offspring," *Child Abuse & Neglect* 28 (2004): 525–545.

71. Letter from former camper shared with Emily Abel and Margaret Nelson, April 21, 2022.

NOTES TO CHAPTER 6

1. Marcia Chatelain, *Growing Up in the Great Migration* (Durham, N.C.: Duke University Press, 2015), 145. This chapter draws heavily on the African American press, which reported camp events in considerable detail. African American newspapers between 1931 and 2003 include *Atlanta Daily World, Baltimore Afro-American, Chicago Defender, Cleveland Call and Post, Los Angeles Sentinel, New York Amsterdam News, Norfolk Journal and Guide, Philadelphia Tribune*, and *Pittsburgh Courier* ("ProQuest Historical African American Newspapers," New York Public Library, accessed October 3, 2021, https://www.nypl.org/collections/articles -databases/proquest-historical-african-american-newspapers). Although mainstream newspapers occasionally reported on events related to African American camps, most accounts appeared in the African American press. For more on this topic, see Emily K. Abel and Margaret K. Nelson, "Integrating Summer Camps," ResearchGate, February 2023, https://www .researchgate.net/publication/368469783_Integrating_Summer_Camps.

2. This source includes some information on the topic: Leslie Paris, *Children's Nature: The Rise of the American Summer Camp* (New York: New York University Press, 2008).

3. Paris.

4. Kenneth B. Webb, "Racial Integration Pays—Financially and in Camp Growth," *Camping Magazine*, April 1961, 10.

5. "Vacation Camps Open," *New York Times*, July 29, 1929.

6. "Negro Camp Authorized," *Baltimore Sun*, May 20, 1944.

7. *Thunderbird*, 1957, 3; "A Camp for 40 Years," *Afro-American*, August 1, 1961; "Tradition of Uniqueness at Camp for Black Kids," *Boston Globe*, August 16, 1982; "Top Camp for Black Americans," *New York Amsterdam News*, August 16, 1980.

8. Brian McCammack, *Landscapes of Hope: Nature and the Great Migration in Chicago* (Cambridge, Mass.: Harvard University Press, 2017), 99–100.

9. William C. Wilson, "Coming Apart: A Case Study of African American Boy Scouts in Northeast, Texas" (master's thesis, Texas A&M University, 2016), 70–71.

10. Elisabeth Israels Perry, "'The Very Best Influence': Josephine Holloway and Girl Scouting in Nashville's African-American Community," *Tennessee Historical Quarterly* 52, no. 2 (Summer 1993): 73–85.

11. "Five-Years Review of Camp E. W. Young," *New Journal and Guide*, August 11, 1951.

12. "Conn. Town Planning Comm. Bars Negro Camp," *Philadelphia Tribune*, June 21, 1955.

13. "Suit Aimed at Park Segregation," *New Journal and Guide*, June 30, 1951.

14. "Summer Camp," *Atlanta Daily World*, August 22, 1959.

15. Kenneth B. Webb, "Racial Integration Pays," 9.

16. Martha M. Verbrugge, "Recreation and Racial Politics in the Young Women's Christian Association of the United States, 1920s–1950s," *International Journal of the History of Sport* 27, no. 7 (May 2010): 1191–1218.

17. Phyllis Palmer, "Recognizing Racial Privilege: White Girls and Boys at National Conference of Christians and Jews Summer Camps, 1957–1974," *Oral History Review* 27, no. 2 (Summer/Fall 2000): 129–154.

18. Thomas J. Sugrue, *Sweet Land of Liberty: The Forgotten Struggle for Civil Rights in the North* (New York: Random House, 2008), 154. See also Martha Biondi, *To Stand and Fight: The Struggle for Civil Rights in Postwar New York City* (Cambridge, Mass.: Harvard University Press, 2003), 82–83. See "Racism at American Pools Isn't New: A Look at a Long History," *New York Times*, August 1, 2018.

19. Michael B. Smith, "'And They Say We Will Have Fun When It Stops Raining': A History of Summer Camps in the United States" (PhD diss., Indiana University, 2002), 146.

20. National Social Welfare Assembly, Education-Recreation Division, "How to Achieve and Maintain Interracial and Intercultural Camping," 1963 Committee on Camping, workshop, box 62, Social Welfare Archives, University of Minnesota.

21. Jessica L. Foley, "'Meeting the Needs of Today's Girl': Youth Organizations and the Making of a Modern Girlhood, 1945–1980" (PhD diss., Brown University, May 2010), 146–147. In 1963, Malcolm Boyd, an Episcopal priest, reported a conversation with Southern White college students. One said, "I attended a camp this past summer in New York that was integrated. I felt that I had to break connection with my Negro friends when I left because I could not invite them to spend the week-end with me at school, go to my home with me or go out to eat in the South" (Malcolm Boyd, "Blind No More," *Pittsburgh Courier*, October 26, 1963). For a later example, see Daryl Khan, "Love in Black and White," Youth Today, June 10, 2013, https://youthtoday.org/2013/06/love-in-black-and-white/.

22. Harry Serotkin, "Experiments in Inter-racial Camping," *Camping Magazine*, May 1944, 12. See "Serotkin to Lead Social Workers," *Pittsburgh Press*, September 6, 1951.

23. McCammack, *Landscapes of Hope*, 186.

24. Ralph Roehm, "Inter-racial Camping—a Successful Experiment in New York State," *Christian Citizenship for Group Leaders* 23, no. 5 (February 1945): 1, 3.

25. "Oppose Limitation in Washington Presbytery," *Atlanta Daily World*, February 19, 1949.

26. "Rev. Asip Attacks Summer Camp Bias," *New York Amsterdam News*, June 13, 1945.

27. Frederic Kernochan, "Letter to the Editor," *New York Times*, May 18, 1934.

28. Chatelain, *Growing Up in the Great Migration*, 147.

29. Serotkin, "Experiments in Inter-racial Camping," 22.

30. Serotkin, 10.

31. Serotkin, 10.

32. Amanda Martin-Hardin, "Nature in Black and White: Summer Camps and Racialized Landscapes in the Photography of Gordon Parks," *Environmental History* 23, no. 3 (2018): 594–595.

33. Marcia Chatelain, *South Side Girls: Growing up in the Great Migration* (Durham, N.C.: Duke University Press, 2015), 148.

34. Felton A. Gibson, "Camp Is a Monument to Interracial Cooperation," *New Journal and Guide*, September 17, 1955.

35. Cathy Hall Bacon, "Camp Aldersgate," *Encyclopedia of Arkansas*, April 17, 2023, https://encyclopediaofarkansas.net/entries/camp-aldersgate-2298/; "Camp History," Camp Aldersgate, accessed March 6, 2021, https://www.campaldersgate.net/about-us/camp-history/; Allie Spensley, "Segregated Summer Camps: The Origins of the American Summer Camp," U.S. History Scene, accessed March 6, 2021, https://ushistoryscene.com/article/segregated-summer-camps/.

36. Sugrue, *Sweet Land of Liberty*, 24.

37. Biondi, *To Stand and Fight*, 6–7.

38. "Lillian Smith Plumps for Interracial Camps," *Afro-American*, April 14, 1951.

39. Mickey Flacks and Dick Flacks, *Making History, Making Blintzes: How Two Red Diaper Babies Found Each Other and Discovered America* (New Brunswick, N.J.: Rutgers University Press, 2018), 61–62; June Levine and Gene Gordon, *Tales of Wo-Chi-Ca: Blacks, Whites, and Reds at Camp* (Avon Springs, 2002); "141 Here from Camp Hit by Polio Get Injections of Gamma Globulin," *New York Times*, June 15, 1953.

40. "Probers Told of Red Camps," *Baltimore Sun*, July 2, 1952.

41. "Five More Refuse to Answer Regarding Communism at Camps at Committee Hearing" [article probably from the Communist *Morgn Freiheit* newspaper], Kheel Center for Labor-Management Documentation and Archives, Martin P. Catherwood Library, Cornell University, Ithaca, N.Y. See Emily Paradise Achtenberg, "'Friends and Neighbors': Remembering Pete Seeger and Camp Woodland," *Monthly Review* 68, no. 4 (January 2015): 15–19.

42. "Tompkins Will Probe Red Camps," *New York Tribune*, July 22, 1955. Kinderland, another Communist camp, came under attack as recently as 2012, when Americans for Limited Government, a conservative organization, revealed that Erica Groshen, President Obama's nominee to the Bureau of Labor Statistics, had sent her children to the camp. The report identified Kinderland's founders as "activists in the Communist Party" and "associated with the left wing of the Workermen's [*sic*] Circle" (Jeffrey Goldberg, "Some Good Old-Fashioned Red-Baiting," *Atlantic*, July, 2012).

43. Kenneth B. Webb, "Racial Integration Pays," 10.

44. Webb, 10.

45. Susan Webb and Kenneth Webb, *Beyond Our Wildest Dreams: The Story of the Farm and Wilderness Camps, 1939–1989*, ed. and designed by Jane Curtis, Will Curtis, and Frank Lieberman (Springfield, Vt.: Springfield Printing Corporation, 1989), 76–77, hereafter *BOWD1989*.

46. Webb and Webb, 72.

47. Diane McWhorter, review of *Subversive Southerner*, by Catherine Fosl, *New York Times*, January 19, 2003.

48. Anne Braden, *The Wall Between* (Knoxville: University of Tennessee Press, 1999); Catherine Fosl, *Subversive Southerner: Anne Braden and the Struggle for Racial Justice in the Cold War South* (New York: Palgrave Macmillan, 2002).

49. Webb and Webb, *BOWD1989*, 74.

50. Encyclopedia of Alabama, s.v. "Clifford Durr," by Sarah Hart Brown, April 8, 2021, http://encyclopediaofalabama.org/article/h-1254.

51. *The WPA Guide to Vermont, the Green Mountain State* (San Antonio: Trinity University Press, 2014). The Webbs were not alone in bringing Black children to Vermont in the late 1940s. A 1948 editorial in the *Rutland Daily Herald* praised Vermonters for "playing host to some 480 youngsters" who arrived through the Fresh Air Fund. The editorial continued that "the hospitality of Vermonters is . . . known. The state that welcomes children into its homes each year is quite in character when it welcomes the Fresh Air Fund youngsters." (The editors did not explain how Vermonters welcomed African American children apart from the Fresh Air Fund.)

52. Cyndy Bittinger, "William J. Anderson," Vermont Public Radio, January 17, 2014.

53. Stephen M. Wrinn, *Civil Rights in the Whitest State: Vermont's Perceptions of Civil Rights, 1945–1968* (Lanham, Md: University Press of America, 1998); Robert L. Walsh, *Through White Eyes: Color and Racism in Vermont* (South Burlington, Vt.: BookSurge, 2006).

54. Walsh, *Through White Eyes*, 55.

55. Kenneth Webb, *As Sparks Fly Upward: The Rationale of the Farm and Wilderness Camps* (Canaan, N.H.: Phoenix, 1973), 153.

56. Webb and Webb, *BOWD1989*, 88.

57. Peg Espinola, Zoom interview with authors, August 20, 2021.

58. Webb, "Racial Integration Pays," 10.

59. Kenneth B. Webb, "Color-Blind Summer Camps," *Nation*, 1949, 494.

60. Webb, 494.

61. Webb, *As Sparks Fly Upward*, 23.

62. Kenneth B. Webb, "Races Mix at Summer Camps," *Christian Science Monitor*, May 26, 1969.

63. Webb, "Racial Integration Pays," 10.

64. Gordon W. Allport, *The Nature of Prejudice* (New York: Perseus Books, 1954), 281.

65. Allan W. Austin, "'Let's Do Away with Walls!' The American Friends Service Committee's Interracial Section and the 1920s United States," *Quaker History* 98, no. 1 (Spring 2009): 5.

66. Ann Scattergood Fogg, Zoom interview with authors, September 9, 2021.

67. Berl Nussbaum, Zoom interview with authors, September 8, 2021.

68. Neil Rolnick, Zoom interview with authors, February 4, 2022.

69. David Finkelhor, Zoom interview with authors, January 13, 2022.

70. Janine Fay, Zoom interview with authors, January 12, 2022.

71. Carol Rapaport Monteleoni, Zoom interview with authors, August 16, 2021.

72. Webb and Webb, *BOWD 1989*, 80.

73. Webb and Webb, 80.

74. "Beyond Civil Rights," US History II (American Yawp), Course Hero, accessed April 23, 2021, https://courses.lumenlearning.com/ushistory2ay/chapter/beyond-civil-rights-2/.

75. "The Civil Rights Movement Continues," US History II (American Yawp), Course Hero, accessed April 23, 2021, https://courses.lumenlearning.com/ushistory2ay/chapter/the-civil -rights-movement-continues-2/.

76. Webb and Webb, *BOWD 1989*, 74.

77. An architect, John Fuller was active in the civil rights movement in the 1950s and 1960s. His wife at the time, Sidney ("Peggy"), was one of a few Unitarian Universalist women who held meetings with Black women in their homes in response to the Birmingham bombings (Gordon D. Gibson, *Southern Witness: Unitarians and Universalists in the Civil Rights Era* [Skinner House, 2015]; "John Merriman Fuller Obituary," *Birmingham News*, July 1, 2011).

78. Webb and Webb, *BOWD 1989*, 75.

79. Howard Frank Mosher, *A Stranger in the Kingdom*, 1st ed. (New York: Doubleday, 1989).

80. Walsh, *Through White Eyes*, 50.

81. Susan Webb, "Integrated Camps," *Rutland Daily Herald*, May 6, 1968, 12.

82. Donzaleigh Abernathy, "Comment," *Rutland Herald*, January 5, 2021, in response to Jim Leddy, "Guess Who Came to Dinner," *Rutland Herald*, December 1, 2020.

83. "Rev. Abernathy, Civil Rights Principal, in Rutland to Visit His Ailing Daughter," *Rutland Daily Herald*, July 9, 1969, 11.

84. Telephone interview with Margaret Nelson, July 15, 2021.

85. Zoom interview with authors, August 27, 2021.

86. Zoom interview with authors, August 7, 2021.

87. "The Anne Shore Sleep-Away Camp Program Celebrates 40 Years with Farm and Wilderness," 1199SEIU Family of Funds, accessed November 4, 2021, https://www.1199seiubenefits .org/news/child-care-and-youth-services-news/anne-shore-camp-40-years/; "Partnerships and Affiliations," Farm & Wilderness, accessed November 4, 2021, https://farmandwilderness .org/about-us/partnerships-affiliations/.

88. Len Cadwallader and Mary Ann Cadwallader, Zoom interview with authors, January 27, 2022.

89. Marc Tracy, "69 Years Later, Philadelphia Apologizes to Jackie Robinson," *New York Times*, April 15, 2016, https://www.nytimes.com/2016/04/15/sports/baseball/philadelphia -apologizes-to-jackie-robinson.html.

NOTES TO CHAPTER 7

1. Morris Kaplan, "150,000 Children Dream of Camps," *New York Times,* June 22, 1958.

2. Advertisement in *Friends Journal,* March 15, 1966, 160.

3. Zoom interview with authors, December 12, 2021.

4. Telephone interview with Margaret Nelson, September 15, 2021.

5. John Trent (pseudonym), Zoom interview with authors, January 5, 2022.

6. In-person interview with Margaret Nelson, August 8, 2021.

7. Telephone interview with Margaret Nelson, August 5, 2021.

8. Ann Scattergood Fogg, Zoom interview with authors, September 9, 2021.

9. Martyne Stout, Zoom interview with authors, September 11, 2021.

10. Mindy Thompson Fullilove, *The House of Joshua: Meditations on Family and Place* (Lincoln: University of Nebraska Press, 1999), 124.

11. John Wilhelm, Zoom interview with authors, September 18, 2021.

12. Zoom interview with authors, August 27, 2021.

13. Telephone interview with Margaret Nelson, March 15, 2022.

14. "How Much Do Teen Summer Jobs Pay per Hour?," ZipRecruiter, accessed September 23, 2022, https://www.ziprecruiter.com/Salaries/Teen-Summer-Salary-per-Hour.

15. Zoom interview with authors, August 27, 2021.

NOTES TO CHAPTER 8

1. Philip J. Deloria, *Playing Indian* (New Haven, Conn.: Yale University Press, 1998), 7.

2. See Abigail A. Van Slyck, *A Manufactured Wilderness: Summer Camps and the Shaping of American Youth, 1890–1960* (Minneapolis: University of Minnesota Press, 2006), 169–214.

3. "Activities," *Thunderbird,* 1958.

4. Reggie Darling, "My Name Is White Rainbow," July 12, 2011, http://reggiedarling.blogspot.com/2011/07/my-name-is-white-rainbow.html.

5. See esp. Deloria, *Playing Indian;* and Shari M. Huhndorf, *Going Native: Indians in the American Cultural Imagination* (Ithaca, N.Y.: Cornell University Press, 2001).

6. See Pauline Turner Strong and Laurie Posner, "Selves in Play: Sports, Scouts, and American Cultural Citizenship," *International Review for the Sociology of Sports* 45, no. 3 (2010): 393.

7. Ernest Thompson Seton, *Two Little Savages: Being the Adventures of Two Boys Who Live as Indians and What They Learned* (New York: Grosset and Dunlap, 1903).

8. Deloria, *Playing Indian,* 96.

9. David Martinez, *Dakota Philosopher: Charles Eastman and American Indian Thought* (St. Paul: Minnesota Historical Society Press, 2009); Kiara M. Vigil, "Charles Eastman's 'School of the Woods': Re-creation Related to Childhood, Race, Gender, and Nation at Camp Oahe," *American Quarterly* 70, no. 1 (March 2018): 25–53.

10. Deloria, *Playing Indian,* 123.

11. Kenneth B. Webb, *Mehrlicht Camp, Plymouth Vermont* (Baltimore: Press of the Hoffman Brothers, 1940), 3.

12. The Mohawk are one of the five original nations of the Iroquois League, now known as the Haudenosaunee.

13. That brook is called "Indian" Brook; it is the source of the name of the girls' camp.

14. "The Indian Village and the Coups," F&W Archives (manuscript shared by Rick Hausman).

15. Barry Wohl, Zoom interview with authors, September 8, 2021.

16. Susan Webb and Kenneth Webb, *Beyond Our Wildest Dreams: The Story of the Farm and Wilderness Camps, 1939–1989* (Springfield, Vt.: Springfield Printing, 1989), 22, hereafter *BOWD1989*.

17. Webb and Webb, 22.

18. Letter from Wakio to Ken Webb, provided by Rick Hausman.

19. Pam Podger, "Captain William Rassenes," Farm & Wilderness, accessed December 28, 2021, https://farmandwilderness.org/tag/captain-william-rassenes/.

20. Leslee Goodman, "Women Are the First Environment: Interview with Mohawk Elder Katsi Cook," *Braided Way: Faces and Voices of Spiritual Practice*, November 3, 2018.

21. Katsi Cook, "Voices of Feminism Oral History Project," interview by Joyce Follet, *Sophia Smith Collection of Women's History*, October 26–27, 2005.

22. "Indian Village and the Coups," *Thunderbird*, n.d.

23. Kenneth B. Webb, *As Sparks Fly Upward: The Rationale of the Farm and Wilderness Camps* (Canaan, N.H.: Phoenix Publishing, 1973), 136.

24. Darren Bonaparte, "Nia:wen ko:wa, Tehanetorens, Akwesasne Remembers Ray Fadden," *Indian Country*, December 26, 2008.

25. Cook, "Voices of Feminism."

26. "Prosperous Year Had by Camp Counselors in Eastern Camps," *Bacone Indian*, September 20, 1931, 31.

27. Leslie Paris, *Children's Nature: The Rise of the American Summer Camp* (New York: New York University Press, 2008), 215.

28. Paris, 215.

29. Deloria, *Playing Indian*, 125.

30. Jack Lord, "Ellsworth Jaeger (1897–1962)," Find a Grave, February 10, 2009, https://www.findagrave.com/memorial/33709420/ellsworth-jaeger.

31. Here, for example, is the information about an Iroquois drum. Jaeger begins by explaining why a camp counselor might want to make that item: "One of the most pleasant drum sounds and yet far reaching too is that of the water drum of the Iroquois." He writes, "To hear the resonant throb in the night forest is to hear the great pulse of prehistory come again to life. The music and dance of 10,000 years is re-awakened in the echoing beats." Jaeger then states, "The water drum is usually made of a hollow cedar or basswood log, chipped until it become a mere shell. The bottom is made watertight with a cross section of a log fitted perfectly and then cemented with spruce gum. In the lower part of the drum a small hole is bored into which is fitted a wooden stopper. The drumhead is made of a piece of soft leather, stretched tightly in place by means of a wooden hoop wrapped with buckskin." Finally, Jaeger provides instructions about the use of the drum: "It must be filled to about a third with water, the drumhead being wet and then partly dried. A small wooden drum stick is used. The drum is usually small, the largest being not more than 12 inches in diameter" (Ellsworth Jaeger, *The Indian Counselor Handbook* [Buffalo: National Youth Administration, State of New York: 1938], 32).

32. According to historian Leslie Paris, campers occasionally discovered that their Indian counselors were conveying alien traditions. Hyman Bogen was "thrilled" when Basil Williams, the Seneca counselor at Camp Watikan, boiled sassafras roots on an overnight night. Bogen was "disappointed," however, when he found Williams consulting a book of Indian tales before the evening campfire. Paris, *Children's Nature*, 215.

33. Cook, "Voices of Feminism."

34. Bob Cochran and Warren Howe, "Indian Lore," *Thunderbird*, 1958.

35. Vincent Schilling, "Boy Scouts 'Have Been One of the Worst Culprits' of Cultural Appropriation," *Indian Country Today*, September 15, 2019; "Mission and Purpose/Order of the Arrow, Boy Scouts of America," Boy Scouts of America, accessed December 20, 2021, https://oa-bsa.org/about/mission-purpose.

36. Barry Wohl, Zoom interview with authors, January 14, 2022.

37. John Bancroft, Zoom interview with authors, September 16, 2021.

38. Telephone interview with Margaret Nelson, August 1, 2021.

39. Berl Nussbaum, Zoom interview with authors, September 8, 2021.

40. "Arthur and Shirley Einhorn Iroquois Collection," St Lawrence University Libraries—Special Collections, Canton, N.Y.

41. "Audio Log—Emily and Rick Hausman, Vermont 1970s, Project Interview," Vermont Historical Society, July 15, 2015, https://www.digitalvermont.org/vt70s/AudioFile1970s-44.

42. Kenneth M. Kline, "Naming Good Path Elk," *Essence* 28, no. 7 (November 1997).

43. Bob and Rick Hausman, Zoom interview with authors, July 28, 2021.

44. "Standing High, Frank," *Rapid City Journal*, July 5, 2017. At the time of his death, he was living in Rapid City, making Native American art for sale and still teaching traditions.

45. Jane Elkington Wohl, "Reflections on Racism at Flying Cloud in the Years '68, '69, '71, '72, and '73," May 24, 2001, letter in the possession of Nate Hausman.

46. Wohl.

47. Sunshine Mathon, Zoom interview with authors, January 9, 2022.

48. After leaving Flying Cloud, Allen Flying By worked at Night Eagle, a camp established in 2000 by Bruce Moreton, a former Flying Cloud director. In December 2007, a jury convicted a man by the name of Allen Flying By of embezzlement and theft from an Indian tribal organization. He was sentenced to thirty-three months and ordered to repay $8,200 (United States of America v. Allen Flying By, No. 07-1076, U.S. App. [8th Cir.]).

49. Wohl, "Reflections on Racism."

50. Nate Hausman, Zoom interview with authors, December 2, 2021.

51. Letter from Nate Hausman to Emily K. Abel and Margaret K. Nelson, December 13, 2021. The Abenaki were Indigenous people who inhabited northeastern Canada and the United States.

52. Webb and Webb, *BOWD 1989*, 25.

53. Deb Haaland, "My Grandparents Were Stolen from Their Families as Children. We Must Learn about This History," *Washington Post*, June 11, 2021.

54. Allan W. Austin, "'Let's Do Away with Walls!' The American Friends Service Committee's Interracial Section and the 1920s United States," *Quaker History* 98, no. 1 (Spring 2009).

55. Kenneth B. Webb, Letter to Editor, *Friends Journal*, February 1, 1969.

56. Webb, *As Sparks Fly Upward*, 133.

57. Arlene B. Hirschfelder, *American Indian Stereotypes in the World of Children: A Reader and Bibliography* (Metuchen, N.J.: Scarecrow Press, 1982); Kendra James, "Guiding in the Wrong Direction: The Problematic, Ongoing History of the Adventure Guides," shondaland, March 12, 2018, https://www.shondaland.com/live/a19381796/guiding-in-the-wrong-direction/.

58. A few institutions did respond to criticisms. After a protest in 1972, for example, the Wooden Indian Bar at the Americana Hotel in New York closed (see Karen Schwartz, "Is Travel Next in the Fight over Who Profits from Native American Culture?," *New York Times*, August 3, 2021). Camp Lincoln, a boys' camp in the Adirondacks, also eliminated its Indian practices (Hallie E. Bond, Joan Jacobs, and Leslie Paris, *"A Paradise for Boys and Girls": Children's Camps in the Adirondacks* [Syracuse, N.Y.: Adirondack Museum / Syracuse University Press, 2006], 76).

59. Bob Hausman and Rick Hausman, Zoom interview with authors, July 18, 2021.

60. "Introductory Notes," in possession of Nate Hausman.
61. Mathon, Zoom interview with authors.
62. Draft of article by Sunshine Mathon to be published in the *Interim*, in the possession of Nate Hausman.
63. Nate Hausman, letter to campers, 2001, in the possession of Nate Hausman.
64. Draft of article to be published in the *Interim*, in the possession of Nate Hausman.
65. Wohl, "Reflections on Racism."
66. Hausman, letter to campers.
67. "Captain William Rassenes," Farm & Wilderness, accessed November 4, 2021, https://www.farmandwilderness.org/news-and-announcements/tag/captain-william-rassenes.
68. Jane Wohl, Zoom interview with authors, January 6, 2022.
69. Sunshine Mathon, article in *Interim*, 2002.
70. Flying Cloud, "A Visit to the Akwesasne Community, a New Partnership with the St. Regis Mohawk Tribe," Farm & Wilderness, December 11, 2019, https://www.farmandwilderness.org/news-and-announcements/2019/12/11/a-visit-to-akwesasne.
71. Katsi Cook, "Voices of Feminism."
72. Goodman, "Women Are the First Environment."
73. Goodman. See also Elizabeth Hoover, "Katsi Cook: 'Research and Ceremonies and Healing Are an Empowerment Process'—a Mohawk Midwife Brings the Needs of Women into Environmental Health Research," in *Junctures in Women's Leadership: Health Care and Public Health*, ed. Mary E. O'Dowd and Ruth Charbonneau (New Brunswick, N.J.: Rutgers University Press, 2021), 1–22.

NOTES TO CONCLUSION

1. Frances McLaughlin, executive director, "Letter to the F&W Community," email message to author, June 1, 2021.
2. Frances McLaughlin, executive director, "Letter to the IB Community at Farm & Wilderness: A Special Camp Message," email, received by Margaret Nelson, August 12, 2022.
3. Centers For Disease Control, "Births and Natality," FastStats, last modified February 23, 2023, https://www.cdc.gov/nchs/fastats/births.htm.
4. "Summer Camp Infographic: Amazing Facts on USA Camps," Regpack, accessed September 12, 2022, https://www.regpacks.com/blog/infographic-amazing-facts-summer-camps-united-states; "The 10 Most Popular Types of Summer Camps for Kids," Kids Camping Essentials, accessed September 12, 2022, https://kidscampingessentials.com/how-to-choose-the-best-summer-camps-for-kids/.

INDEX

Page numbers in *italics* refer to figures.

ABOUT THE AUTHORS

EMILY K. ABEL is professor emerita at the Fielding-UCLA School of Public Health. She is the author of many books, including *Tuberculosis and the Politics of Exclusion: A History of Public Health and Migration to Los Angeles* (Rutgers University Press, 2007) and *Elder Care in Crisis: How the Social Safety Net Fails Families.*

MARGARET K. NELSON is A. Barton Hepburn Professor Emerita of Sociology at Middlebury College in Middlebury, Vermont. Most recently, she is the author of *Like Family: Narratives of Fictive Kinship* (Rutgers University Press, 2020) and *Keeping Family Secrets: Shame and Silence in Memoirs from the 1950s.*

Together, they have also authored *Limited Choices: Mable Jones, a Black Children's Nurse in a Northern White Household.*